NAHC
Wild Game Cookbook

Published by the North American Hunting Club
Minneapolis, Minnesota

Acknowledgements

We would like to thank the following for their help:

NAHC Members, for sending us those delicious, original wild
game recipes that serve as the foundation of the 1995 NAHC
Wild Game Cookbook. These recipes — recommended by
your fellow NAHC Members — are certain to delight.

Chef Ron Bohnert and the Native Game Company, for supply-
ing mouth-watering wild game meals and information about
the healthy aspects of eating your favorite wild game.

Artist Larry Anderson, for his wonderfully accurate and stim-
ulating renditions of the game animals and fowl that grace
the various pages of this cookbook.

NAHC staff members, for their diligence, patience and hard
work in seeing to the preparation of a useful and readable
cookbook of which the NAHC's members can be proud.
They include Vice President of Product Marketing Mike Vail,
Marketing Manager of Books Cal Franklin, Project
Coordinator Sherry Bania and Asst. Art Director Ken Kaiser
who created the design. And thanks to freelancer Ron Larsen
for overseeing the production of this cookbook.

*Please address reprint requests
and orders for additional cookbooks to:*
NAHC Cookbook Editor
P.O. Box 3401
Minneapolis, MN 55343

Library of Congress Catalog Card Number 84-649847

ISBN 0-914697-60-9
Copyright 1995, North American Hunting Club

Printed in U.S.A.

2 3 4 5 6 7 8

Contents

Enlightened Dining

by Bill Miller

Not too many North American hunters have heard of the nilgai. And, unfortunately, fewer have hunted them. They're great game and great table fare.

The nilgai is an antelope native to India. It was brought to this country in the first half of this century as an agricultural experiment. Nilgai are large animals (bulls weigh up to 800 pounds) and their meat is superb.

With all that going for it, some entrepreneurial Texans decided the nilgai might be marketable as livestock. What they didn't figure correctly was how wild nilgai are. The animals could not be domesticated. Today, there is a growing wild population on several ranches along the southern Texas gulf coast.

As guide John Frankson with Amos Dewitt's Tio Moya Outfitters described the nilgai, "They're so difficult to approach because they live charged on adrenalin all the time."

Considering the size and tenacity of a nilgai, it might be difficult to understand the disposition toward running first and asking questions later. Even cow nilgai (sometimes jokingly called "nil-gals") weigh about 300 pounds. Hide on a mature bull is more than an inch thick, and their skeletal structure outclasses any elk.

But when you think about it, nilgai wildness is not difficult to understand. In India their primary function is as tiger food. In Texas, they can be hunted year-round, and their heavy-duty build makes them about the best test around for big bore rifle ammunition. If those were two of my main attributes in life, I'd be fidgety, too.

Now this isn't a dissertation on the nilgai—which as you might be able to tell, I love to hunt—but it is an essay on eating light and eating right on wild game. And a plate christened with nilgai steaks or burger is exactly that: light eating, right eating. Nilgai is lower in fat and cholesterol than most any other wild game readily available to the North American hunter. I'll put a nilgai in the freezer for my family at every opportunity.

As Executive Director of the North American Hunting Club, Editor of North American Hunter, and host of "North American Outdoors" on ESPN, I get to hunt more than a lot of folks, it's fair to say. It also means I probably get to eat a lot more wild-game meals than most, too.

It's no stretch of the truth to say that my wife and I buy less than 20 pounds of domestically produced red meat each year. We do buy some chicken, but that's mostly because we quickly go through what the possession limits allow us to have in the freezer in the way of waterfowl and upland birds at the close of the seasons. Whenever my luck is running really good, wild turkey adorns our Easter and Thanksgiving table.

And believe me, we aren't living off the game because we have to—there are a number of deserving charities which already receive any wild game meat more than we believe we'll eat before next season. I'd give them more if we didn't rely on it for the lion's share of our meat.

In my family we eat wild game because we choose to. We like it. We like the flavor, and we utilize dozens of recipes from the NAHC's Wild Game Cookbooks to provide variety. We believe it's part of a healthy diet—low in fat and low in cholesterol. We believe eating wild game is truly "enlightened dining."

Because I try to cut home fuel bills by heating at least part of the time with a wood stove, I know well the adage that good firewood you make yourself heats you at least four times: when you cut it, when you split it, when you stack it and when you burn it! Relying on wild game for a large portion of your day-to-day diet is much the same. It keeps you physically fit at least three times: when you prepare for the hunt, when you are hunting and when you eat it!

Enjoying enlightened dining on wild game doesn't call for fancy recipes, heavy sauces, overcooking or lots of work. In fact, one of my family's favorites is as simple as it gets. Wild game steaks (caribou, nilgai, moose, deer, elk—whatever I was fortunate enough to take in the fall) are thawed and go on the grill. I season generously with black pepper and lightly with garlic salt. Cook to medium rare. Eat with baked potatoes (light on the butter for "enlightened dining"), sauteed mushrooms and a lettuce salad or corn on the cob if it's in season. We eat that meal at least once a week year-round. And we often serve it to guests—none of whom have ever turned a nose skyward and most of whom get real quiet because they're too busy eating to talk. It's a meal which is that easy, that light and that good.

Eating right and eating light, and truly enjoying wild game are certainly reasons enough to make wild game a major component in your family's diet. But there's another that is vitally important. The idea that hunters take great care to utilize the meat from the animals they take is crucially important to the public image of hunting. While we'll never be able to defend hunting in the modern world solely from the aspect that it puts meat on the table, this reason for hunting is an important one to the non-hunting public.

And if you need one more reason to make wild game part of your enlightened diet, how about that it just plain tastes great. Who besides a North American hunter could say he's tried musk-ox, nilgai and wild boar chop suey. I have, and it is darn good!

To all fellow enlightened diners of the North American Hunting Club, take care and good hunting. Then enjoy the results in your heart and at the table.

Bill

Bill Miller
Executive Director

Game Meat, The Healthy Choice

When the settlers moved westward across the plains and mountains of what was to become the United States of America, they didn't realize at the time that living off the land by harvesting game was a pretty healthy thing to do. Of course, at the time they didn't have much choice because grocery stores were few and far between. But the choice they had was a good one.

Today, we live in a world of *super* supermarkets which provide for our every want and need in terms of food—for a price. Today's hunter, however, has discovered that the game he or she harvests is at least equal to, and in many cases better than the domestic meats that are available in the markets in terms of fat content and cholesterol levels. Not only that, but wild game meat is just darn good eating.

There are a number of reasons why the healthy aspects of wild game are such a well-kept secret, primarily because wild game meats haven't really interested nutritionists much. They've been concentrating on the red meats and fowl that normally show up on the local supermarket's refrigerated shelves. But the recent trend in restaurants toward offering more wild game meats has led to a new-found awareness of the healthy aspects of wild game foods.

We at NAHC are the first to admit that the average hunter, when drawing a bead on a magnificent trophy elk, probably isn't thinking at the moment that it will yield a 3.5-ounce roast with only 1.9 grams of fat, 146 calories and 73 milligrams of cholesterol! No sir. It probably will be upon reflecting on a savory roast dinner that the thought will occur to our hunter. Nor does he know that a 3.5-ounce serving of roasted moose yields less than 1 gram of fat, 134 calories and 78 milligrams of cholesterol.

Well, those are numbers, but what do they mean? According to the USDA, here are the figures for the same sized serving of top

9

How game meats compare

Meat	Fat grams	Cholesterol milligrams	Calories
Beef, top loin, broiled	9.6	76	209
Chicken, light meat, skin removed, roasted	4.5	85	173
Antelope, roasted	2.6	126	150
Bison, roasted	2.4	82	143
Deer, roasted	3.2	112	158
Duck, domesticated, skin removed, roasted	11.2	89	201
Duck, wild, breast meat, raw	4.25	n/a	123
Elk, roasted	1.9	73	146
Moose, roasted	<1	78	134
Pheasant, breast meat, raw	3.2	n/a	133
Quail, breast meat, raw	3	n/a	123
Rabbit, domesticated, roasted	6.3	64	154
Rabbit, wild, roasted	3.5	123	173
Squirrel, roasted	3.6	95	136

All estimates based on a 3.5 oz. serving.

Source: USDA Handbook Series No. 8   Linda Smith/Argus Leader

loin beef, broiled: 9.6 grams of fat, 76 milligrams of cholesterol and 209 calories! And for chicken (light meat roasted with skin removed): 4.5 fat grams, 76 milligrams of cholesterol and 173 calories.

Venison is significantly more nutritious than beef. A 3.5-ounce serving of roast yields 3.2 grams of fat and 158 calories, although venison is slightly higher in cholesterol than beef. Still, overall not a bad choice, but a hunter with an eight-pointer in his sights probably isn't thinking that deer are less fatty than chickens.

If you were unable to bag a deer, elk or moose last season, don't despair. An excellent alternative is probably hopping through your garden at this very moment. Yes, the rabbit. According to the USDA, it has more protein, less fat and fewer calories than any of the other domestic meats: chicken, veal, turkey, lamb, beef or pork. Rabbit meat checks out at 20.8 percent protein, 10.2 percent fat and 795 calories per pound of uncooked meat. Turkey and chicken are the closest to rabbit in protein content, and chicken is the closest competitor in percent of fat and number of calories. Rabbit meat is pearly white, tender, juicy, mild in flavor, nutritious and appetizing.

And don't overlook squirrels. A 3.5-ounce serving of squirrel yields 3.6 grams of fat, 95 milligrams of cholesterol and 136 calories.

Another major contender among the larger animals was once considered big game. That's the buffalo, or bison if you prefer. Because it now leads a rather sedentary life in small herds, the buffalo is a little higher than elk and moose in fat and cholesterol, but it ranks very favorably against beef in all three categories. A 3.5-ounce serving of buffalo meat contains 2.4 grams of fat, 82 milligrams of cholesterol and 143 calories, and it ranks high along with rabbit in protein percentage.

Waterfowl and upland game birds such as pheasant and quail rank along with deer in amount of fat, which is well below chicken. Wild ducks are healthier fare than chicken at only 4.25 grams of fat per 3.5-ounce serving, and only 123 calories compared with 173 for the same-sized serving of chicken.

By now, you're probably getting the picture on the healthy side of all of our delicious wild game meats which should be a part of every American's diet. The healthy aspects of your wild game harvest are another reason to enjoy your hunting experience and the feast that follows!

Cookbook Abbreviations

tsp. = teaspoon
T = tablespoon
pt. = pint
oz. = ounce
pkg. = package
qt. = quart

Measurement Conversions

1 pinch = less than $1/8$ tsp.
1 T. = 3 tsp.
2 T. = 1 oz.
4 T. = $1/4$ cup
5 T. + 1 tsp. = $2/3$ cup
8 T. = $1/2$ cup
10 T. + 2 tsp. = $2/3$ cup
12 T = $3/4$ cup
16 T. = 1 cup

1 cup = 8 oz.
1 pint = 16 oz.
1 quart = 32 oz.
1 gallon = 128 oz.

1 cup = $1/2$ pint
2 cups = 1 pint
4 cups = 1 quart
2 pints = 1 quart
4 pints = $1/2$ gallon
8 pints = 1 gallon
4 quarts = 1 gallon
8 gallons = 1 bushel

Meet The Chef!

For healthy, delicious wild game meals the whole family will enjoy, we turned to Ron Bohnert, Senior Executive Chef of one of the largest Radisson Hotels in the country. Ron is also the Corporate Chef for the Native Game Company, a large supplier of wild game meats to hotels, restaurants and resorts worldwide. You'll find four of Ron's favorite wild game meals (including appetizer, main course and dessert), starting on the next page.

In preparing wild game, Ron says it's "all in how it's handled." It must be treated gently as if it's an egg—you don't want to over-marinate and definitely not over-cook any of your game products. He prefers a simplistic approach to game and fish preparation, "like our great-grandparents, but with a modern day flair in the sauce or with just the right garnish."

Chef Ron has prepared pheasant, duck, wild boar, elk, caribou, venison, black bear, rattlesnake as well as many large saltwater and freshwater fish dishes ... sometimes for two people and sometimes for 2,000! His culinary travels have taken him throughout the Midwest and Western states, British Columbia and as far away as Ocho Rios, Jamaica.

Throughout his career, Ron has participated in many culinary competitions. Some of the many highlights include his second place award at the 1st Annual Wild Game Cook Off for his Pan Seared Peppered Pheasant Breast with a Dried Cherry Port Sauce. (This award-winning recipe is the foundation of his second meal in this book.) He also has received Best of Show, Silver Medal and Bronze Medal in the American Culinary Federation Food Competition, and the People's Choice Award from the Minnesota Pork Producers. Ron was also chosen the Host Chef for the 1992 Superbowl.

We're excited about Ron's involvement in this edition of the North American Hunting Club Wild Game Cookbook. His high-protein, lower fat dishes are top rate. Enjoy!

Wild Game Dinner No. 1
Venison Steak Dinner
Game Spice Blend
BBQ Rabbit Appetizer
with Corn Bread Sticks and Honey Butter
Grilled Potatoes with Olive Oil and Fresh Basil
Charcoal Grilled Venison Steak
with Roasted Garlic Burgundy Butter

Game Spice Blend

1	**cup fresh rosemary, chopped**
1	**cup thyme, chopped**
1	**cup granulated garlic**
1/2	**cup coarse black pepper**
1/2	**cup salt**

Use this delicious spice blend on any game meat.

BBQ Rabbit

1	**each whole rabbit, cut into 6 serving pieces: boneless loins, front and hind quarters and thighs**
2	**T. olive oil**
1	**T. garlic salt**
1	**T. lemon pepper**
1/2	**T. black pepper**
1/2	**T. fresh thyme**
2	**cups of your favorite BBQ sauce, mixed with 1/2 cup honey for great flavor**

Mix together salt, lemon pepper, black pepper, and thyme. Place rabbit in bowl, sprinkle with spice blend and olive oil, let rest at room temperature for 30 minutes, or 3-4 hours in refrigerator.

Over hot charcoals on grate, place rabbit on grill, mark on both sides. Cook 5-7 minutes, then brush with BBQ sauce on both sides, cook until tender, brushing with BBQ sauce until desired doneness - about 10-15 minutes. Do not overcook loins.

Roasted Garlic

Cut garlic bulb in half. Brush with olive oil and place cut-side down on charcoal broiler away from direct heat, comparable to 350° oven. Cook until tender, about 10-15 minutes. Pop out cloves and enjoy.

Garlic Burgundy Butter

1/2 bulb roasted garlic clove, finely chopped
1 each shallots, finely chopped
2 cups burgundy
1 cup butter, chilled (cut in small pieces)

In saucepan, add burgundy, garlic and shallots. Reduce by 1/2, remove from heat. Whisk in chilled butter, season with salt and pepper. Serve with venison steaks.

Grilled Potatoes with Basil

1 lb. russet potatoes, sliced about 1/4-inch thick
2 T. olive oil
1 cup fresh basil, finely chopped, reserve half for later use
1 T. garlic salt
1 T. Italian seasoning

Toss sliced potatoes in olive oil, then add ½ of basil, garlic salt and Italian seasoning.

Place potatoes on broiler, cook on one side until light brown, then turn them over and cook until tender. Place in bowl, toss with remaining half of basil and serve.

15

Grilled Venison Steak

4 each 12-16 oz. venison steaks, rinsed and patted dry
2 T. olive oil – brush on steaks
1 T. Game Spice Blend per steak, generously sprinkled

Broil over high heat, turning once or twice to color the steaks. For 1 1/2 inch steaks, 2-3 minutes per side. Remember once you pull the steaks off the broiler, they continue to cook. Venison steaks are best enjoyed when medium rare.

Wild Game Dinner No. 2
Pheasant Breast Dinner
Wild Mushrooms, Fresh Herbs
and Oven Dried Tomatoes with Fettucine
Pan Seared Peppered Pheasant Breast with Dried
Cherry, Balsamic Vinegar and Port Wine Sauce
Wild Berry Crumble

Wild Mushrooms, Fresh Herbs and Oven Dried Tomatoes with Fettuccine

2   cups wild mushrooms - shitake, morel, trumpet, portabella or any combination, washed and cut in strips
3   T. fresh marjoram, chopped
2   T. fresh thyme, chopped
3   T. fresh garlic, minced
2   cups oven dried tomatoes, cut in strips
3   T. olive oil
I   cup game stock or chicken stock
4   cups cooked egg fettuccini
    salt, cracked pepper
I   pkg. Enoki mushrooms for garnish (optional)

In a sauté pan, heat olive oil and saute minced garlic, wild mushrooms, add fettuccini, tomatoes, fresh herbs, salt and pepper. Toss. Cook for 2-3 minutes to blend flavors, add stock and cook for 2-3 more minutes, adjust seasoning and serve. Garnish with fresh herb sprigs, Enoki mushrooms and shredded Parmesan.

Oven Dried Tomatoes

fresh tomatoes, cored and sliced 1/4-inch thick

Place on sheet tray in 275-degree oven and let bake until dry. Remove from tray, let cool. Store covered in refrigerator.

Dried Cherry, Balsamic Vinegar and Port Wine Sauce

1	cup dried cherries
1/3	cup Roland balsamic vinegar
2	cups Sandeman port wine
1 1/2	cup pheasant demi-glace
2	T. unsalted butter, chilled

Simmer cherries in port wine. When cherries are plump, reserve 1/4 cup for garnish. Add Balsamic vinegar; simmer 2-3 minutes. Remove from heat. Add to pheasant demi-glace. Puree with food processor. Place back on stove. Bring to simmer and skim. Fold in chilled butter.

Place sauce on bottom of plate; slice pheasant breast into five slices. Fan out on top of sauce. Granish with Enoki mushrooms, fresh thyme sprig, croquette potatoes shaped like mushrooms; add the reserved dried cherries.

Pan Seared Peppered Pheasant Breast

4   **each pheasant breasts, boned, skin on, wing joint attached**
3   **T. five peppercorn blend, coarsely ground**
1/4   **tsp. salt**

Rinse pheasants and tap dry. Rub with peppercorn mixture and salt. In a hot, heavy bottomed pan, sear pheasant breasts on skin side first; turn over and sear bottom. Place pheasant breasts on hot plate and place in 350-degree oven until medium rare (120-degree internal temperature). Remove from oven; keep warm until plating. Reserve leg and thighs for making smoked pheasant meat for another use. Reserve carcass for pheasant demi-glace.

Wild Berry Crumble

3   **cups each raspberries, blueberries, strawberries, blackberries**
1/2   **cup sugar**
2   **T. lemon juice**
3   **T. flour**

Mix above ingredients. Place in buttered glass baking dish.

1   **cup flour**
1   **cup brown sugar**
1   **cup quick cooking oatmeal**
1   **cup butter, chilled and cut small**

Mix well until a coarse mixture. Sprinkle on top of berry mixture. Place in preheated 350-degree oven, bake until crisp, 20-25 minutes. Serve with your favorite vanilla ice cream or frozen yogurt.

Wild Game Dinner No. 3
Country-Style Venison Roast Dinner
Wild Rice Nut Salad with Cranberry Vinaigrette
Country-Style Venison Roast with Onions, Carrots
with Garlic Whipped Potatoes

Wild Rice Nut Salad with Cranberry Vinaigrette

1 1/2   cups uncooked wild rice
4 1/2   cups water
1 1/2   tsp. salt
        black pepper to taste, freshly ground
        Cranberry Vinaigrette
1   cup mushrooms, sliced
1/2   cup celery, sliced
1/4   cup green onions, sliced
1/2   cup red cabbage, coarsely shredded
1   cup mixed nuts (walnuts, cashews, pecans, almonds, sun flower seeds or any combination)
2   cups cooked chicken, duck, pheasant or wild turkey (optional)

Wash rice in cold running water until water runs clear. Bring water to boil. Add salt. Pour in rice all at once and return to rapid boil. Stir once with fork. Cover pan and reduce heat to low. Cook for 20 minutes or until grains puff and are tender but slightly chewy. Season with pepper. Prepare Cranberry Vinaigrette. Mix chilled wild rice and vinaigrette with remaining ingredients.

Cranberry Vinaigrette
(Serves 4)

1 cup cranberry sauce	1 tsp. salt
1/4 cup white vinegar	1 tsp. pepper
2 T. sugar	1 tsp. thyme, ground
1/4 cup salad oil	
1 T. Worcestershire sauce	1 tsp. oregano, ground

Combine all ingredients and mix well. Store in refrigerator in covered jar.

Garlic Whipped Potatoes

- 4 each russet potatoes, peeled
- 1 each roasted garlic bulb, minced
- 2 tsp. granulated garlic
- 1/4 stick butter
- 1-2 cups cream
  salt and pepper to taste

Boil potatoes until tender, drain, then place minced garlic in bowl, add potatoes and whip until smooth. Add butter, cream, and season to taste.

Country-Style Venison Roast with Onions, Carrots and Garlic-Whipped Potatoes

2	T. bacon fat or salad oil
1	3-4 lb. venison roast
2-3	T. game spice
2	cups carrots, cut in 1-inch pieces
2	cups onions, cut in 1-inch pieces
4	garlic cloves, minced
1	cup dry red wine
2	cups beef or game stock

Preheat oven to 375 degrees, heat bacon fat or oil in a heavy oven-proof roasting pan over medium heat. Season venison with one half of spice mixture, sear on all sides, add garlic, vegetables, and remaining spice blend. Place in oven and roast until medium rare or an internal temperature of 110 degrees. Remove meat and vegetables and place on serving platter. Add red wine to roasting pan, deglaze, reduce by one half, add beef or game stock. Bring to simmer, skim, and adjust seasoning. Slice venison roast, place on serving bowl platter with vegetables and garlic-whipped potatoes, garnish with fresh rosemary sprig.

Wild Game Dinners
Substitute Recipes

Wild Rice Potato Pancakes

2	cups cooked wild rice
1/2	cup onions, finely diced
2	cups cooked peeled potatoes
4	each whole eggs
	salt and pepper to taste
1/2	cup fresh basil, cut in strips

Put potatoes in bowl and mash, add remaining ingredients. Fold together, adjust seasoning. Form into patties and saute in olive oil or bacon fat until golden brown. Place on paper towel and keep warm, repeat with remaining mix.

Honey Glazed Carrots

4   cups fresh carrots, peeled and stem removed
2   T. whole butter
2   T. honey
I   T. fresh dill, chopped

Cut carrots diagonally and simmer in salted water until tender. Drain water. Add butter and honey, cook until coated with mixture, sprinkle with dill and serve.

Sautéed Duck Breasts with Cranberry Vinaigrette

4   each duck breasts, boned, skinned and fat removed
I   T. olive oil
I   T. fresh thyme, chopped
    salt and pepper

Rinse duck breasts and pat dry. Sprinkle seasoning on both sides of breast. Heat a sauté pan over high heat. Add olive oil, then duck breast, sear on both sides. Reduce heat to medium and continue to cook until medium rare, about 4 minutes. They should feel springy to the touch. Add cranberry vinaigrette, bring to a boil, then remove from heat. Remove duck, slice in three and fan out on serving plate. Place cranberry vinaigrette over breast. Place two wild rice pancakes, carrots and then garnish with fresh herb sprig.

Chocolate Espresso Torte

- I   lb. unsalted butter
- I   cup + I T. sugar
- I   cup brewed espresso coffee
- I   lb. bittersweet chocolate, chopped
- 6   whole eggs, room temperature
- 6   egg yolks, room temperature

Preheat oven to 325 degrees. Place kitchen parchment paper in the bottom of a 12-inch springform pan. Butter and dust with flour.

In a heavy saucepan, over low heat, melt butter with sugar and espresso. Stir until sugar dissolves. Add chocolate and cook until mixture is smooth. Remove from heat.

In a large bowl, whisk eggs and egg yolks until frothy. Whisk into chocolate. Pour into pan. Bake about 1 hour or until edges puff slightly and crack, but center is not set. Cool. Makes one 12-inch torte.

Big Game

Deer

Babbit's Venison Stir-Fry

1	lb. venison steak or roast, cut in thin slices
4	T. oil
4	celery stalks, thinly sliced
2	carrots, thinly sliced
2	onions, sliced and separated
2	green peppers, cut into chunks
2	pkgs. stir-fry seasoning mixes (sweet and sour is best with venison)
1/4	cup water
8	fresh mushrooms, sliced

Heat oil in wok or large skillet over high heat until hot. Brown meat in hot oil. Stir-fry for about 2-3 minutes or until meat is brown. Add celery, carrots, onions and green pepper. Stir-fry for 2 minutes or until tender-crisp. Mix seasoning mixes in 1/4 cup water. Blend well. Add mushrooms to wok and cook for 1 minute. Stir in seasoning mixture. Cook and stir until sauce thickens and vegetables are glazed. Serve with rice.

Tim Babbitt
Kalamazoo, Michigan

Dan's Mexican Chili Con Carne

6	lbs. prime venison (top and bottom round, boned)
4	medium onions, chopped
I	large head garlic, minced
24	chile de arbol entero (dry chili pods)
10	jalapeno peppers
1/2	lb. butter
I	T. oregano, basil, ground cuminos
I	T. turmeric, paprika, cayenne pepper
I	cup water
I	8-oz. can tomato paste
4	cans whole peeled tomatoes
	salt to taste

Chop onions, garlic, chilis and peppers. Add to melted butter in an 8-qt. pot. Cook for 15 minutes. Add meat strips chopped to 1-inch squares and brown. Add spices, 1 cup water and tomato paste. Stir frequently. Break up tomatoes and add to chili. Cook for 1-6 hours. Add salt to taste. Serve with tortillas or bread.

Daniel J. Clark
Endwell, New York

Bill's Venison Jerky

2	lbs. venison
3/4	cup teriyaki
3/4	cup Worcestershire sauce
1/2	bottle of liquid smoke
2	tsp. seasoning salt
2	tsp. Accent
2	tsp. onion powder
1 1/2	tsp. garlic powder
1	tsp. black pepper

Slice venison into thin strips. Place all ingredients, except meat, into bowl and mix. Add meat to mixture, cover and marinate for 24-48 hours. Place a cookie sheet in bottom of oven to catch drippings. Place toothpicks through one end of meat, then hang toothpicks across upper oven rack so meat will hang down between bars. Heat oven to lowest setting, cook for 8-12 hours or until dry.

Bill Milligan
Yucca Valley, California

Beer Deer Chops

4-6 chops
      oil
      flour
1 can imported beer
1 can white hominy

Brown chops in oil and flour. Remove meat. Add beer and hominy to meat juices, stir until thick. More flour may be added to thicken if necessary. Return meat to pan, cover and cook on low until done, approximately 20-30 minutes.

Bill Milligan
Yucca Valley, California

Influencing Flavor, Tenderness

The flavor and tenderness of venison is greatly affected by age and other factors. Here's a simple test to assess the quality of your animal. The first thing to cook from your deer is a round steak. A round steak recipe is a good way to show you how the rest of the cuts will taste and you won't waste a really choice cut in the process. You can cook the rest of your animal with the knowledge in hand that you gained from the round steak and make necessary adjustments in your recipes to compensate for any stronger flavors or tougher-than-expected meat.

Lemon/Lime Deer Steak

1-2 **deer steaks**
1/2 **lemon**
1/2 **lime**
1 **bottle of your favorite Italian dressing**

Tenderize steaks, place in shallow dish. Squeeze juice from lemon and lime over steaks. Add 1/2 to 3/4 bottle of dressing. Marinate steaks for 24 hours. Barbecue over medium heat for 5-8 minutes per side, depending on thickness.

Bill Milligan
Yucca Valley, California

Serve It Hot!

Always serve venison hot. Plan your meals so that everyone is sitting at the table ready to eat when the venison is finished cooking. Using hot plates to serve on will help.

Buttermilk Venison Pot Roast

5   lbs. venison
1/2 lb. onions
2   T. vinegar
1/2 pint sour or buttermilk
1/2 pint water
2   cinnamon sticks

Brown venison in pan, season as desired, add onions, vinegar, milk, water and cinnamon sticks. Cover tightly and bring to a boil. Reduce heat and simmer on stove or in slow oven (300 degrees for 2 hours or until tender). Turn meat 2 or 3 times while cooking. Add liquid as needed.

Bill Milligan
Yucca Valley, California

Under-Cooking Helps

When cooking venison, under-cooking slightly should be your goal. When over-cooked, it's dry and tough and the flavor tends to slip away.

Nimrod's Ugly Buck Jerky

3-4	lbs. meat
1/4-1/2	cup water
5	oz. soy sauce)
2	T. steak sauce
6	T. Worcestershire sauce
2	tsp. hickory-flavored salt
2	tsp. Accent
1	tsp. pepper
1/2	tsp. salt
1	tsp. lemon pepper seasoning salt

Cut meat into strips, 1/8-inch thick by 3/4-inch wide. Mix sauce ingredients well. Pour over meat and coat well. Refrigerate overnight (12 hours or more). Drain meat. Sprinkle with lemon pepper seasoning on both sides. Place drip pan under meat in oven. Hang strips on oven rack with toothpicks. Bake at 140 to 150 degrees for 5-6 hours or until meat is dried (but not brittle). Bake with oven door open 3 inches. (Recipe will work for all wild game — deer, elk, turkey, caribou, pronghorn, moose, antelope.)

Kevin G. Holly
Dillsburg, Pennsylvania

Heart, Tongue and Kidney Pie

Pie Filling:
1 venison heart
1 venison tongue
2 venison kidneys
3 carrots, diced diagonally
5 small potatoes, sliced
10 mushrooms, sliced
1 large onion, quartered, slivered and broken apart
1-2 tsp. sage
salt and pepper to taste

Roux:
4 T. butter
4 T. flour (thickening)

Broth:
1 celery stick with leaves
1 carrot, roughly chopped
2 cloves
2 bay leaves
1 medium onion, quartered
3 sprigs parsley
1 tsp. salt
10 black peppercorns
20 whole coriander seeds

Crust:
1 egg, mixed with 1 tsp. water and beaten
2 pie crust sticks

Wash heart. Cut out fat, veins and arteries. Remove outer membrane of kidneys. Split open and remove all fat and white veins. Soak kidneys in cold salted water for 30 minutes. Rinse tongue. Place all broth ingredients and meat in heavy 4-qt. pot. Bring to boil, cover, and simmer for 1 1/2 hours. Remove meat from broth; strain and reserve about 3 cups broth. When meat cools, remove skin from tongue; and chop the meat into 1/4-inch to 1/2-inch chunks. Prepare roux. Mix butter and flour over low heat, stirring until golden brown in color. Add 3 cups broth, and blend.

Make 2-crust pie, following directions on package. Put all ingredients in pie shell — diced meats on the bottom. Pour in gravy (roux), sprinkle with salt, pepper and sage. Seal and flute crust. Brush with egg and water mixture. Leftover dough can be used to make designs on crust. Brush again with egg mixture. Place pie in preheated oven (325 degrees) and bake for 1 hour.

Jim and Suzi Hundemer
La Plata, Maryland

Any-Way Burritos (with Venison)

1	lb. ground venison	1	7¹/₂ oz. can tomatoes, cut up or 1 8-oz. can stewed tomatoes
15-20	flour tortillas		
1	onion, chopped		
2	garlic cloves, minced	2	8-oz. cans tomato sauce
4	T. all-purpose flour		
2	T. chili powder	3	cups cheddar cheese, shredded
2	4-oz. cans mushrooms		

Stack tortillas; wrap in foil. Heat in 350-degree oven for 10 minutes to soften. In large skillet cook meat, onion, and garlic until meat is brown. Drain off fat; stir in flour, chili powder, mushrooms, tomatoes and tomato sauce. Cook and stir until thick and bubbly, until tomatoes and mushrooms are tender. Spoon about 1/3 cup of filling onto each tortilla just below the center. Top each with 2 T. of cheese, fold bottom edges up and over, just to cover the filling. Fold in opposite sides, just until they meet. Roll up tortillas from bottom. Fry, bake or microwave rolls as desired.

Fry: Secure rolls with toothpick. In 1 inch oil, fry 3 at a time for 1-2 minutes; on each side or until crisp and golden. Drain. Place rolls, seam side down on ungreased baking sheet, uncovered. Bake at 375 degrees for 15-25 minutes.

Microwave: Place 4 rolls on plate. Cover with paper towel. Cook for 1-2 minutes or until hot. Filling can also be used for tacos.

Tim Babbitt
Kalamazoo, Michigan

Back Strap Stuffed Venison

 1   piece of back strap, 8 inches long
 1/4 cup cider vinegar
 3   T. olive oil
     salt and pepper
 2   fresh garlic cloves, crushed tarragon
 1   onion, chopped fine
 1/4 lb. bleu cheese
 1/2 cup red wine

Marinate back strap in vinegar, olive oil, salt, pepper, crushed garlic and a little tarragon, for 2 hours in the refrigerator. Remove. Beginning about one inch from either end, slice the strap almost all the way through, forming a pocket in the meat. Mix together one onion, bleu cheese, more salt and pepper. Pack mixture into pocket of meat. With opening upward, pour in 1/2 cup red wine. Close opening with wooden toothpicks or bamboo skewers. Wrap in foil (opening side up) and cook in a 350-degree oven for 1 hour (time depends on thickness of meat). To serve, cut in slices, arrange on platter, pour melted cheese from foil over the top.

Ronald M. Tussel, Jr.
Hawley, Pennsylvania

Shanked Venison

  1   **venison shank per person**
1/4 **cup peanut oil**
  2   **garlic cloves, crushed**
      salt and pepper
      red wine
      small whole potatoes
      fresh carrots
  2   **T. flour for gravy**

Heat peanut oil, add garlic. Lightly brown garlic and remove. Salt and pepper the browned shanks on all sides. Add two inches red wine to pressure cooker. Arrange small whole potatoes and fresh carrots around the outside edges of pot, with shanks in the middle. Cover meat with potatoes and carrots also. Bring to pressure and cook for about 1/2 hour. Arrange on platter, shanks centered, surrounded by vegetables Mix 2 T. flour with cold water, add to pan juice to thicken gravy, pour over serving. Serve with steaming biscuits.

Ronald M. Tussel, Jr.
Hawley, Pennsylvania

Black Hills Buck in Beer

    3   lbs. venison cut into 1-inch cubes
    2   T. flour
 1 1/2 tsp. salt
 dash   pepper
   1/2 tsp. dried rosemary
    4   medium onions, sliced and separated into rings
    1   garlic clove, minced
    1   small bay leaf
    3   whole cloves
   12   oz. beer
    2   T. red wine vinegar
    1   tsp. dijon mustard

Best done in a clay cooker. Soak top and bottom in water for 30 minutes before cooking. Coat meat with flour, salt, pepper and rosemary and place deer meat in cooker; or brown meat with these ingredients, if using casserole. Stir in onions, garlic, bay leaf and cloves. Pour over meat. Place covered cooker in cold oven. Set oven at 425 degrees. Bake, stirring once or twice until deer is very tender (2 1/2 to 3 hours).

Stir beer, vinegar and mustard into meat mixture. Garnish with parsley if desired. Serve with broad noodles and crusty bread.

French Onion Steak in a Crock

2   lbs. venison steak (or elk)
    flour
    salt
    pepper
    garlic powder
    oil
2   pkgs. onion soup
4   cups water
    potatoes, sliced
    carrots, sliced

Coat steak with flour, salt, pepper, garlic powder. Fry thin steak in flour, using hot oil. Brown both sides well. Place in Crockpot. Mix onion soup mix with 4 cups of water. Pour over steaks, cook on high 5 hours. You can add potatoes or carrots in the last 2 hours of cooking.

Kip L. Osterhout
Hazelton, Indiana

Anything Goes With Venison

Serve your venison with just about any vegetable or potato, just like beef.

Sandy's "Souper" Yummy

2   lbs. ground venison
    noodles
1   can cream of mushroom soup
1   can creamy chicken mushroom soup
    salt and pepper to taste
    butter

Make 6-8 small patties, about 3 inches in diameter.
Brown well on both sides. Drain excess fat. While patties are browning, boil water for noodles. While noodles are cooking, combine the soups, salt and pepper
to taste in a separate pan. Stir to blend the soups,
reduce to simmer until noodles are done. Drain the
noodles and add a little butter to reduce sticking.
Serve the patties on the side and the soup/gravy over
the noodles.

John and Sandy Ralte
Mira Loma, California

Easier Meat Handling

When forming patties from ground meat,
if you dip your hands in cold water before
handling the meat, it won't stick to
your fingers.

Sarge's Venison Meatballs and Gravy

Meatballs:
- 10 lbs. ground venison
- 4 lbs. sweet sausage
- 2 fist-sized onions, finely chopped
- 10 large eggs
- 3 cups bread crumbs
- 2 T. salt
- 1 T. black pepper
- 1 tsp. ground cloves
- 1 tsp. nutmeg
- 4 T. garlic in oil, minced

Mix meat and sausage. Spread out mixture to 1-inch thick. Combine remainder of ingredients, spread over meat mixture, and mix by hand, kneading and folding into meat mixture. Roll into small meatballs (wet hands work best for rolling meatballs). Brown in oil of choice.

Gravy:
- 2 26-oz. cans cream of mushroom soup
- 2 26-oz. cans water
- 8 beef bouillon cubes
- 3 T. red hot or Tabasco sauce
- 3 T. Worcestershire sauce
- 1/2 cup dark corn syrup or pancake syrup

Mix all ingredients. Bring to low boil, then simmer with lid on for 1 hour. Put cooked meatballs into gravy, and simmer covered for 1 hour. Makes 300-400 meatballs.

"Sarge"
W. Paterson, New Jersey

Magic Meat Loaf

  2 lbs. venison, coarsely ground
  1 egg
  1/2 cup green pepper, chopped
  1/2 cup onion, chopped
  1/2 tsp. salt
  1 cup cracker crumbs
  1 packet brown gravy mix (7/8 oz.)
  1 cup milk
  4-6 small potatoes, cut up, unpeeled

Mix all ingredients, except for potatoes, in large bowl. Shape into loaf. Place in Crockpot. Place potatoes around the sides of loaf. If potatoes are peeled, wrap in foil to keep from darkening. Cover and cook on low for 8-10 hours. Can also be cooked on high for 5 hours.

Amelia Bragg
Waverly, Ohio

Nutrition Label
What it means

Extra Lean: Less than 5 grams of fat, 2 grams of saturated fat and 95 milligrams of cholesterol per serving.

Sharon's Deer Steaks

I	lb. deer steaks
I	can golden mushroom soup
$^1/_4$	cup onion
$^1/_4$-$^1/_2$	cup water

Brown meat, then place in Crockpot. Mix soup and onions and add to Crockpot. Add water. Cook on medium until tender. Serve over rice with salad.

Freezing Meat Whole

Any large cut of meat that you plan to cut into steaks should be frozen whole. If you cut the meat into steaks before freezing, moisture will escape from the meat quicker. If you're using the meat as stew meat or grinding it for burger, it is best to follow this tip. Each cut surface is a potential escape route for moisture in the meat. Every bit of moisture you can retain will improve the meat when cooked.

Brother K's Venison Tenderloin

1-2	lbs. venison tenderloin
	salt
	pepper
1/4-1/2	cup Worcestershire sauce
	red wine (optional)
2	garlic cloves
	oil
	flour
1	can condensed cream of mushroom soup
1	cup milk

Season venison with salt and pepper. Marinate in Worcestershire sauce and wine, if desired, for 2 hours (save marinade sauce). Crush garlic cloves and sauté in hot oil. Roll venison steaks in flour and brown in oil. Mix cream of mushroom soup with milk and add to leftover marinade. Place browned steaks into baking dish and pour soup mixture over meat to coat. Cover with foil or lid and bake at 350 degrees for 45 minutes in preheated oven. Serve with noodles or rice.

K.K. Sethna
Ashville, Ohio

Sriracha Salami

2 lbs. ground venison
1 cup water
2 T. Morton curing salt
1 T. black pepper
1/2 T. garlic powder
1/2 T. mustard powder
1 T. mustard seed
1 T. sriracha sauce
2 T. liquid smoke

Mix all ingredients together in large plastic or glass bowl. Form into 2 log rolls. Wrap in waxed paper and refrigerate for 24-48 hours. Bake for 3 hours at 250 degrees on an open rack. Place cookie sheet underneath to catch any drippings.

Terry Tantlinger
New Kensington, Pennsylvania

Nutrition Label
What it means

Light (Lite): One-third fewer calories or no more than half the fat of the higher-caloric, higher-fat version, or no more than one-half the sodium of the higher sodium version.

Grilled Venison Chops

1 **venison backstrap, cut into boneless chops**
  Italian dressing
  Worcestershire sauce
  lemon pepper to taste
  salt to taste
  bacon

Marinade: Cover boneless chops with equal parts of Italian dressing and Worcestershire sauce. Refrigerate overnight. Remove chops from marinade. Keep remaining marinade for basting. Add lemon pepper and salt to taste. Take strips of bacon and wrap around chops. Hold in place with toothpicks (1 strip per chop). Place on hot grill. When turning, baste with marinade. For added flavor, use charcoal grill.

Barney D. Holland
Wrightsville, Georgia

**Nutrition Label
What it means**

Fat Free: Less than 0.5 gram of
fat per serving.

Juleen's Marinated Deer Meat

Marinade:
  1   soy sauce
 1/2 cup lemon juice
      flour to coat
      garlic, minced
      shortening

Store in refrigerator. Marinate meat in soy sauce and lemon juice for a few hours. To fry, place deer meat in soy sauce, then cover with flour. Place meat in frying pan with butter-flavored shortening and garlic; fry at 300 degrees until thoroughly cooked.

Juleen Stammen
Palermo, North Dakota

Restrained Marinade Use

Use marinades with restraint, they can be overpowering if meat is allowed to stand in the marinade for a long time. Always follow the recipe, but consider substituting any lightly acidic liquid such as lemon juice or tomato juice. These will tenderize the meat without imparting strong tastes. A good substitute for marinating is to s-s-s-l-l-l-o-o-o--w-w-w cook instead.

Angelia's Deer Meatballs

1	lb. deer hamburger
1	cup green onions
1/2	cup white onions
1	cup green peppers
1/4	cup garlic
1	egg
	milk
	flour
	shortening
	salt
	pepper

Mix hamburger, onions, peppers and garlic. Mix in egg. In two separate containers, place flour in one and milk in the other. Form meat mixture into meatballs the thickness of your choice. Heat shortening on medium heat in a deep, heavy skillet. Dip each meatball into the milk, then the flour and cook in the hot oil until done. Salt and pepper to taste.

Angelia M. LaKey
Booneville, North Carolina

North Carolina Deer Stew

3-5 lbs. deer roast
1 cup vinegar
  water
2 cups beef stock
1/2 tsp. black pepper
1/4 cup Worcestershire sauce
1 large onion, sliced
1 medium green pepper, diced
3 medium potatoes, cut 1/2-inch thick

In Crockpot, soak roast in vinegar and cover rest of roast with water. Let meat cook overnight on low heat. Pour out vinegar and water. Add beef stock, black pepper and Worcestershire sauce, then cover roast with water. Cook for 3 hours. Add onions, green peppers and potatoes to meat. Cook until tender.

Angelia M. LaKey
Booneville, North Carolina

Barney's Tenderized Venison Steaks

8-10 venison steaks, tenderized
 2-3 cups milk
      lemon pepper and salt to taste
   1 cup flour
      cooking oil
   1 can cream of mushroom soup
   1 medium onion, cut into rings

Soak venison steaks in milk overnight. Wash thoroughly and pat dry. Season steaks with lemon pepper and salt. Dredge steaks in flour and brown on all sides. Cook in oil until inside of steak turns white. Do not over-cook. Move steaks to a baking dish. Blend 1 can of cream of mushroom soup with 1 can of water. Pour over steaks. Place onion rings on top of steaks. Cover dish with foil and bake until tender. Serve with vegetables or baked potato and salad.

Barney D. Holland
Wrightsville, Georgia

Barbecued Venison

3-4 **lbs. roast, boneless**
vinegar
water

Soak meat in 1 part vinegar and 3 parts water for 1 hour. Roast in oven at 350 degrees until fully cooked, then chop meat.

Barbecue Sauce:
  I   **cup vinegar**
  2   **tsp. Worcestershire sauce**
I 1/2 **tsp. chili powder**
  I   **T. paprika**
  I   **T. salt**
  I   **T. lemon juice**
  I   **T. brown sugar**
  I   **T. butter**
  I   **T. catsup**

Combine sauce ingredients and bring to boil. Pour over chopped meat and heat in 325-degree oven for 15 minutes.

Wayne's Jerky

6-8	**lbs. chuck roast**
25	**oz. Worcestershire sauce**
I	**oz. garlic powder**
1/2	**oz. onion powder**
2-4	**oz. tabasco sauce**

Mix ingredients (except meat) in large bowl. Cut roast in 1/4-inch strips, trimming off excess fat. Cutting is easier if meat is partially frozen. Soak meat in bowl overnight, for about 10 hours. Put toothpicks through ends of strips.

Place cookie sheet on oven bottom to catch drips. Hang meat strips on top rack of oven.

Set oven at 150 degrees and bake for 15-20 hours with oven door cracked open a little to allow moisture to escape.

Wayne Warner
South Zanesville, Ohio

Homemade Deer Salami

4	lbs. deer hamburger
1/2	lb. ground pork
1/4	cup Morton's Tender Quick Salt
2	T. liquid hickory smoke
2	tsp. black pepper
2	tsp. garlic powder
1	tsp. seasoning salt
1	tsp. paprika
1	tsp. mustard seed
	peppercorns (whole black pepper)

Mix hamburger, pork and quick salt thoroughly. Refrigerate overnight. Add in remaining ingredients, mix well. Divide in half, make two rolls.

Put in pan on lower oven rack (second from bottom). Bake at 225 degrees for 4 hours. Let cool.

Dennis J. Ratosky, Sr.
Portage, Pennsylvania

Bagged Deer

3-4 lbs. venison
1/2 cup flour
1 8-oz. can tomato sauce
1/2 cup water, or favorite wine
1 tsp. instant beef bouillon
1/4 tsp. pepper
4 red potatoes, halved
3 carrots, quartered
3 celery stalks, cut into 2-inch pieces
12 mushrooms, halved

Marinate roast in your favorite marinade overnight. Shake flour into cooking bag and place bag into a 13x9x2-inch baking pan. Add tomato sauce, water or wine, instant bouillon and pepper. Squeeze bag to mix ingredients. Place roast in the center of bag and place the veggies around the roast. Close the bag with the tie provided. Cut about 6 1/2-inch slits in top of bag. Bake for 2 to 2 1/2 hours in preheated 350-degree oven.

David B. Roman
Chicago, Illinois

Savory Venison Sauté

1/2	lb. ground venison
1	T. pine nuts
1	tsp. olive oil
2	garlic cloves, minced
1/2	cup onion, chopped
2	eggs
1 1/2	T. sumach
	salt and pepper to taste
2	cups fresh spinach, coarsely chopped

In a frying pan or toaster oven, roast the pine nuts to a light golden brown, then set aside. In a nonstick skillet, heat the olive oil on medium, then add garlic and onions. Cook for 1 minute. Add venison and cook until halfway done (about 6 minutes), stirring continuously. Break 2 eggs over the meat mixture, sprinkle with sumach (a cinnamon-color Middle Eastern seasoning), salt, pepper, and top with the spinach. Cover the skillet and cook the mixture for 4 minutes, until the spinach is lightly steamed. Remove cover, add the toasted pine nuts and stir. Continue cooking until meat is done. Serve rolled in hot flour tortillas or pita bread.

Terry Stevenson
Leadville, Ohio

Gene's Broiled Venison Fillets

4 **venison fillets, cut 1-inch thick**
olive oil
Kitchen Bouquet
garlic salt
black pepper
2 **T. Parmesan cheese**
2 **tsp. mayonnaise**
Tabasco sauce

Rub olive oil on each side of fillets, then brush on a very small amount of Kitchen Bouquet. Sprinkle with garlic salt and black pepper. Broil 3 minutes on one side, then 2 minutes on the other (for rare meat). Remove pan from the oven and brush each steak with a mixture of Parmesan cheese, mayonnaise and a few dashes of Tabasco sauce. Return meat to oven and broil an additional minute, until the cheese is just melted and starting to turn golden. Serve immediately.

Terry Stevenson
Leadville, Ohio

Leda-Style Venison

1	lb. venison, sliced 3/8-inch thick (loin is best)
1/2	cup milk
2	eggs
1/2	T. salt
1/2	T. pepper
1	cup Italian bread crumbs (or regular with Italian seasoning)

Tenderize meat on cutting board, until thin. Combine milk, eggs, salt and pepper in bowl. Spread bread crumbs on deep plate. Dip meat in milk and egg bowl, then coat with bread crumbs. Drop in deep fat at 325 degrees. Meat will float when done, or leave in longer to reach desired brownness.

Wayne G. Betterton
Nathalie, Virginia

Frozen Venison

The maximum freezing period for lean venison is no more than one year, and for venison burger and sausage three to four months. Body organs shouldn't remain frozen for more than three months.

Breaded Venison with Mushrooms and Wine

4-6 venison steak, 1/4-inch-1/2-inch thick
1/2 cup flour
1 T. cooking oil or margarine
1/2 cup onion, chopped
1 4-oz. can of mushrooms
1 cup wine
  salt and pepper to taste

Coat meat with seasoned flour and brown in oil in a heavy skillet. Add onions, mushrooms and wine. Salt and pepper to taste. Cook over medium heat for 20-30 minutes.

H.G. "Doug" Douglas
Huntsville, Arkansas

Adding Salt Properly

Here's another trick to keep your game meat as moist as possible. If adding salt to meat, do so at the end of the cooking time. Salt draws moisture out while the meat is cooking.

Pat's Perfect Loin

2-3 **lbs. venison tenderloin, sliced 1/4-inch thick**
salt
pepper
Maggi seasoning
1/2 **stick butter or margarine**
1/2 **cup mushrooms, sliced (optional)**
2 **onions, sliced**

Salt and pepper venison to taste. Apply 6-8 dashes of Maggi seasoning to venison. Melt butter in frying pan. Fry venison, mushrooms and onions together slowly over a low flame, for 5-10 minutes per side. Turn and season opposite side. Serve on bread or roll as a sub, or with potatoes and other side dishes.

Walter and Pat Geschel
Baltimore, Maryland

**Nutrition Label
What it means**

Low Fat: Three grams of fat (or less) per serving.

Venison Roast While You Work

I   **venison roast, thawed**
    salt and pepper to taste
I   **large onion, sliced**
I   **pkg. dry onion soup mix**
I   **can sauerkraut or cut cabbage**
    buttered mashed potatoes

Spray large Crockpot with cooking spray. Place roast
on bottom of pot. Add salt and pepper. Add water
until roast is 1/2 covered. Place onion slices on roast.
Sprinkle 1 package of dry onion soup mix over pot.
Add sauerkraut or cabbage over roast. Cook on low for
8-9 hours.

If necessary, increase temperature to high for last hour.
Serve with sauerkraut over buttered mashed potatoes.
Include onion soup or broth. Other vegetables may
be used.

Tom Vath
Johnston, Iowa

Venison Bologna

12	lbs. ground venison
4	lbs. ground beef
16	T. Tender Quick
8	tsp. liquid smoke
1	tsp. garlic powder
2	cups water
	dry ground hot peppers (optional)

Mix all ingredients together well. Refrigerate for 24 hours. Fill bologna casings. Bake on broiler pan for 1 hour at 350 degrees.

George R. Danner
Etters, Pennsylvania

Freezers Dry Out Meat

You probably have a frost-free freezer at home where you will be storing a lot of your game meat. Frost-free freezers remove the moisture from everything in them, including your hard-earned game.
This makes it doubly important to wrap meat at least twice (preferably 3 times) before freezing.

Italian-Style Venison

> venison, cut into bite-sized pieces
> olive oil
1 garlic clove, sliced
2-3 hot cherry peppers with juice
> mushrooms
> rosemary
1 cup white vinegar

Pour olive oil in pan to cover the bottom. Slice up garlic clove and heat until the garlic begins to turn brown. Add venison pieces, cherry peppers, and some juice from the pepper jar. Add mushrooms and a touch of rosemary.

Cover and let simmer, stirring occasionally, until the juice is almost completely absorbed. Add vinegar and let simmer until the vinegar is almost gone.

Richard Trost
Vernon, New York

Gary's Deer Stew

1   ham or 2 shoulders from deer, or about a 10 lb.
     roast
     water to cover meat in a 20-qt. pot
2   packets of beef stew seasoning mix
2   T. hot sauce
1   T. garlic salt
1   T. Italian seasoning
     salt and pepper to taste
1   5-lb. bag of potatoes, peeled and cut in about
     1-inch cubes
1   bag of carrots, cut 1-inch long
1   bunch of celery, cut 1-inch long
8-10 medium onions, quartered
     cornstarch

Boil meat in water with beef stew seasoning mix, hot
sauce, garlic salt, Italian seasoning, salt and pepper.
Boil until meat falls off bone. Remove bone. Add vegetables and cook for 1 hour or until vegetables are
done. Thicken with cornstarch mixture (cornstarch
thoroughly mixed with cool water). Serve over rice.

Gary R. Pierce
Ellabell, Georgia

Patty's Venison Goulash

1-2 lbs. venison, cut into cubes
1 onion, sliced and quartered
2 garlic cloves, minced
   olive oil
1 1/2 cup water
3/4 cup catsup
2 T. Worcestershire sauce
1 T. brown sugar, packed
2 tsp. salt
2 tsp. paprika
1/2 tsp. dry mustard
   cayenne pepper to taste
1/4 cup cold water
2 T. flour

Sauté venison, onion and garlic in olive oil until meat is brown. Drain off oil. Add remaining ingredients (except flour and water) and simmer 2 1/2 to 3 hours. Mix cold water and flour in shaker, add to venison mix. Heat to boiling and boil for about 1 minute. Serve over noodles.

Patty Pryts
North Huntington, Pennsylvania

Venison Fillets in Rotel Sauce

12 venison fillets
 1 can Rotel (tomatoes diced with green chilis)
 1 cup sour cream
 1 can cream of mushroom soup
 2 cups flour
 1/2 tsp. garlic powder
 1/2 tsp. sage
 1/2 tsp. oregano
     salt and pepper to taste
     cooking oil

Mix Rotel, sour cream and cream of mushroom soup, blend well and set aside. Mix flour and spices, then dredge filets in mixture. Brown fillets in skillet in hot oil.

Drain and place in baking dish. Pour Rotel mixture over fillets. Bake at 350 degrees for 1 hour.

Steve Strickbine
Bartlesville, Oklahoma

Murphy's Roast

3-4 lbs. venison roast (or moose, elk)
6-8 medium-sized potatoes, peeled
4-6 medium-sized onions, peeled
8-10 carrots, peeled and cut 6-inch long
1 pkg. Lipton's dry onion soup mix
or dry vegetable soup mix
1/4 cup water or dry white wine

Place roast, potatoes, onions and carrots in a cooking bag, then put in a roasting pan. Mix dry soup with water or wine; pour over roast and vegetables. Close bag with twister. Puncture small hole in top of bag.

Cook at 325 degrees for 1 to 1½ hours or until done. Remove roast and veggies from bag and strain liquid for au jus gravy.

Mike Murphy
Wallingford, Vermont

Buck & Beans

2   lbs. ground venison
1   large Vidalia onion, chopped very fine
    salt and pepper to taste
2   16-oz. cans pinto beans

Place chopped onions and ground venison into large iron skillet. Salt and pepper to taste. Brown meat on high heat until all pink is gone. Add Luck's pinto beans from can, and cover. Cook on low heat approximately for 30 minutes.

Ray R. Clevenger
Gadsden, Alabama

**Nutrition Label
What it means**

Reduced or Less Fat:
At least 25 percent less fat per serving
than the higher-fat version.

Venison Wellington

2-3	lbs. venison tenderloin or backstrap
4	T. vegetable oil
I	tsp. black pepper
1/2	tsp. oregano
1/2	cup mushrooms, finely chopped
I	medium onion, finely chopped
I	clove garlic, smashed
4	T. butter
I	pkg. of puff pastry
I	egg

Rub oil on tenderloin, season with pepper, oregano, and any other of your favorite herbs. Place in roasting pan and roast in preheated oven (450 degrees) for 20-25 minutes. Cool. Sauté mushrooms, onions and garlic in butter until onions are transparent. Cool. Roll puff pastry on floured board until large enough to completely go around tenderloin. Place loin on pastry to one side and cover with onion and mushrooms mix. Roll loin up in pastry stopping 1 inch short. Brush edges with water and fold ends to seal, with the seam on bottom. Brush with beaten egg. Bake in preheated oven (450 degrees) for 20-30 minutes. Cut in 1/4-inch slices to serve.

Brandie J. Iverson
Saltspring Island, British Columbia, Canada

Pete's Pressure Pot Pleaser

3   lbs. venison, cut into stew or hamburger meat
1   T. cooking oil
3   large potatoes, peeled and sliced
4   carrots, sliced
3   celery stalks, diced
1   onion, diced
1   11-oz. can corn with juice
1   11-oz. can peas or lima beans with juice
1   11-oz. can mushrooms with juice
1   11-oz. can stewed tomatoes
1/2   cup red wine
1   bay leaf or your favorite seasoning
1/2   tsp. pepper
1/2   tsp. salt (optional)
1/2   cup barley

Fry venison in cooking oil until brown. Add all the above ingredients. Add water to cover all, but pot should be no more than 3/4 full. Put lid on, "rocker" over vent. Heat at high temperature until "rocker" starts "rocking;" reduce temperature to low heat for 20 minutes. Turn heat off and let the pot cool and pressure dissipate. Pouring cold water over the pot will also cause the pressure to drop quickly . Do not remove lid until "rocker" is removed and pressure has dropped to normal.

Pete Cuipenski
New Port Richey, Florida

Meatballs in Wine

I	lb. venison hamburger
I	apple, pared and cored
I	small onion
I	egg
1/2	tsp. salt
1/2	tsp. poultry seasoning
dash	pepper
I	cup bread crumbs
2	cups light red wine

Combine apple, onion and egg in blender until liquified. Add to meat with seasoning and bread crumbs.

Mix well and form into balls the size of a nickel. Brown in shortening, drain fat, and add wine.

Simmer for 30 minutes and serve hot.

S.C. Weihert
Wausau, Wisconsin

Wisconsin Deerburgers

I	lb. ground venison
I	small onion, chopped
I	T. chili sauce
I	celery stalk, chopped
I	carrot, ground

Mix all ingredients together. Form into thick patties and fry in a heavy skillet. Brown patties on both sides, turning only once. Cover and cook until done.

S.C. Weihert
Wausau, Wisconsin

Once Is Enough

When you're cooking hamburgers from your favorite wild game meat, cook each side only once. Never mash a burger while it's cooking.

Venison Stew

1 ½ lbs. venison, elk or moose, cut into
    1-inch cubes
 2 cups flour seasoned with salt and pepper
 3 T. oil
 1 medium onion, chopped
 1 celery rib, chopped
 1 beef bouillon cube
1 ½ cups water
 ½ tsp. thyme
 5 drops Tabasco sauce
 4 large carrots, cut into 1-inch chunks
 4 medium potatoes, cut into 1-inch chunks

Mix flour with salt and pepper to taste. Heat oil in a large frying pan. Coat meat with flour mixture and brown on all sides. Add onion, celery, bouillon cube, water, thyme and Tabasco sauce to the pan and stir until boiling, then cover and simmer for about 1 hour. Add carrots and potatoes, plus a little more water if needed.

Cover and cook until vegetables are tender. Thicken broth with flour and season with salt and pepper to taste. Serve hot.

Carl Bartelt
Hillsboro, Wisconsin

Barbecued Venison or Elk Roast

3 lbs. venison (or elk) meat

Marinade:
- **1/3 cup olive oil**
- **1/3 cup light soy sauce**
- **1/3 cup tomato juice**
- **1/3 cup brown sugar**
- **3-4 garlic cloves, minced**

Combine ingredients and marinate meat for 24 hours, turning the meat occasionally. After the meat has marinated, place in a preheated kettle barbecue and cook at 145 degrees, using indirect heat (about 14 pieces of charcoal on each side) for about 1 hour for a 3-lb. roast (medium rare). Do not overcook! Let stand 5 minutes before slicing.

Terry Stevenson
Leadville, Colorado

Howdy's Secret Deer Steak Marinade

4-5 deer steaks
1 medium-sized bottle Italian salad dressing
2 T. McCormick's Cajun Black Powder steak sauce
3 T. lemon juice
2 T. soy sauce

Place deer steaks on bottom of Tupperware container. Mix ingredients and pour over top of steaks. Cover, then shake for 1 minute. Let marinate 18 hours. Fry or grill, brushing with leftover marinade sauce.

Howard W. Reges, Jr.
Butler, Pennsylvania

Sure-Fire Breading Tip

Here's a fool-proof recipe for breading almost anything from meat to vegetables. After cutting your food into pieces, dry them off with paper towels. Then cover with flour, dip in beaten egg (coating completely), then roll in bread crumbs. Let the food pieces dry for about 10 minutes before cooking. It works every time!

Aunt Phyllis's Venison Roast

2-3	lbs. deer roast
3	T. butter
1	T. instant onion
1/2	tsp. garlic powder
1/2	tsp. chili powder
1	tsp. salt
1	tsp. pepper
2	T. flour
1/2	cup burgundy

Mix ingredients to make a paste. Rub on sides and top of roast. Place roast on a sheet of foil and pour burgundy over roast. Cover and seal foil.

Cook at 350 degrees for 2 1/2 to 3 hours. Pour off juice for gravy.

Gary Estlund
Clarkston, Washington

Venison Steak and Gravy

1 1/2-2 lbs. venison steak, roast or chops
 1/4 cup flour
 1 envelope brown gravy mix
 1 envelope onion soup mix
 1 12-oz. can of beer

Trim fat from steak. Cut steak into serving-sized pieces. Dip in flour and set aside. Combine remaining flour and ingredients. Cook all in Crockpot on low heat for about 10 to 12 hours. Makes excellent gravy for potatoes or rice.

Roy Koeller
Green Bay, Wisconsin

**Nutrition Label
What it means**

Lean: Less than 10 grams of fat, 4 grams of saturated fat and 95 milligrams of cholesterol per serving.

Bite-Sized Tamales

I	lb. ground venison
I	lb. ground pork
I	cup V-8 juice
4	eggs
2¹/₂	T. chili powder
2	tsp. garlic powder
2	cups yellow cornmeal
¹/₂	cup all-purpose flour
I	tsp. seasoning salt
I³/₄	tsp. ground cumin
2¹/₂	tsp. paprika
¹/₂	tsp. cayenne pepper

Salsa:

2	16-oz. cans stewed tomatoes
2	tsp. seasoning salt
I ¹/₂	T. chili powder
¹/₂	tsp. oregano

Preheat oven to 350 degrees. Combine venison, pork, V-8 juice and eggs in large mixing bowl. Blend well. In separate bowl, combine chili powder, garlic powder, cornmeal, flour, seasoning salt, cumin, paprika, and cayenne pepper. Mix dry ingredients into meat mixture. Roll into bite-sized balls. Place tamale balls into two 13x9-inch pans. Bake for 30 minutes. Remove from oven and drain. To make salsa, place tomatoes in non-aluminum saucepan. Stir in seasoning salt, chili powder and oregano. Bring to boil, then simmer for 30 minutes. Place tomato sauce in large serving dish. Add tamale balls.

Adam Braune
San Antonio, Texas

Venison in Crockpot

4-5	lbs. venison butterfly steaks or chops cut into 2-inch x 2-inch pieces
2	big peppers, chopped
1	large onion (baseball size), diced
1/2	lb. butter
	flour (Wondra)
1	10-1/2 oz. can consomme
1	8-oz. bottle of cooking sherry
	oregano

Steam or fry peppers and onions. Remove from heat and set aside. Melt 1 stick of butter in large skillet. Pound meat pieces to about 1/4-inch x 1/2-inch thickness with meat mallet. Coat meat in flour. Place in hot pan with butter. Turn 4 times while cooking (meat should be cooked but not dried out); add more butter as needed. Place cooked meat in Crockpot with peppers and onions. Pour consommé and cooking sherry into pan with meat juices and butter. Add pinch of oregano. When hot, pour mixture into Crockpot. Simmer on low for 3 hours or more.

Dale T. Gray, Jr.
E. Stroudsburg, Pennsylvania

Atomic Beans

1-2   lbs. ground venison or venison sausage
3   medium onions, sliced
2   lbs. link sausage cut into 1/2-inch pieces
1   gallon pork and beans
1   jar hot salsa (use mild if preferred)
1   cup of catsup
1/2   cup brown sugar (optional)

Cook ground meat, onions and link sausage in iron pot until done. Add beans, salsa, catsup and brown sugar. Cook for 1 hour.

Gary R. Pierce
Ellabell, Georgia

**Nutrition Label
What it means**

Extra Lean: Less than 5 grams of fat, 2 grams of saturated fat and 95 milligrams of cholesterol per serving.

Best-Ever Sausage

25 lbs. venison (antelope or elk)
25 lbs. pork trimmings
1 1/2 oz. sodium nitrate cure
4 oz. brown sugar
2 oz. black pepper
1 oz. mustard seed
1/2 oz. paprika
4 garlic cloves
1 lb. pickling salt

Coarse-grind meats. Dissolve sodium nitrate in one quart water. Mix spices into ground meat, add cure. Put garlic and 1 cup water in blender and finely chop. Mix meat well and refrigerate 24 hours. Stuff meat into pork casings and place in smoker.

Smoke at 170 degrees until casings begin to drip or turn cherry red.

John Kouba
Beach, North Dakota

Chorizo (Mexican sausage)

1½   lbs. venison, coarse ground
1   lb. ground pork
3-4 cloves garlic, ground or chopped to taste
     vinegar
     salt to taste
     oregano to taste
3-4 red chili pods

Grind meats and combine. Blend garlic, vinegar and spices well. Add mixture to meat and mix well. Wash chili pods, boil and drain.

Art Dalmolin
Reedsport, Oregon

Nutrition Label
What it means

Low in Saturated Fat: One gram saturated fat (or less) per serving and not more than 15 percent of calories from saturated fatty acids.

Todd's Venison Stir-Fry

10 oz. venison, cut in thin strips
4 T. soy sauce
2 T. cold water
2 T. corn starch
2 T. olive oil
1 1-lb. bag stir-fry vegetables

Marinate venison in 1 T. soy sauce for about 1 hour. Cook venison in 1 T. hot oil in wok at 350 degrees until the inside of the meat is just pink.

Remove meat, add the rest of the oil and cook the vegetables with the rest of the soy sauce for 3 minutes, or until vegetables are tender.

Mix with venison and serve. Serve with rice or noodles.

Todd Gebert
Sheboygan, Wisconsin

Venison Roast and Garlic

    5   lbs. roast
    6   garlic cloves, diced
  1/4   cup olive oil
  5-6   cups water
    3   large onions, sliced
    3   T. butter or margarine
    I   14-oz. can mushrooms
    2   cups cooking sherry
    I   T. cornstarch
        salt and pepper to taste

Sauté garlic in olive oil, using a pot large enough for the roast. After garlic is browned, add roast and brown on all sides. Add water and cook on medium heat, until roast begins to fall apart (3-4 hours). Slice onions and sauté in frying pan. Add butter and mushrooms. Sauté until soft. Add to roast. Mix sherry and corn-starch with a little warm water, add to roast. Stir until thick. Salt and pepper to taste. Serve over mashed potatoes or noodles.

David Miller
Tampa, Florida

Zesty Venison Stew

3	lbs. venison, cubed
3	T. flour
3	T. +1 tsp. chili powder
1	tsp salt
1	T. paprika
3	T. cooking oil (virgin olive)
1	garlic clove, crushed
2	large yellow onions, sliced
1	30-oz. can tomatoes
1/2	tsp. crushed hot peppers
1	big splash Tabasco sauce
1	tsp. cinnamon
1/2	tsp. cloves powder
1	tsp. celery flakes or 1 stalk cut into 1-inch pieces
1	beef bouillon cube, crushed
1 1/2	cups water
1	dozen peppercorns
2	cups carrots, cut into bite-sized chunks
2 1/2	cups potatoes, cut into 2-inch chunks

Mix 2 T. flour, 1 tsp. chili powder, salt and paprika. Coat venison cubes and brown in cooking oil in large Dutch oven. Flavor enhancing lard may be used. Toss in garlic and onion until cooked, about 10 minutes. Add tomatoes, crushed peppers, Tabasco, 3 T. chili powder, cinnamon, cloves and celery. Simmer with lid on for 2 hours. Add water occasionally, if necessary. Mix bouillon and 1 1/2 cups water (or a 10-oz. can of beef bouillon) with 1 T flour. Add to pot. Add peppercorns, carrots and potatoes; cook 30 minutes.

Ralph J. Bridge
Stamford, Connecticut

Swiss Venison Loaf

1 1/2 lbs. ground venison
  1 egg
  1/2 cup evaporated milk
  1 tsp. sage
  1 tsp. salt
  1/2 tsp. black pepper
  1 cup crackers
  3/4 cup Swiss cheese
  1 envelope Lipton onion soup mix
2-3 strips bacon

Preheat oven to 350 degrees. Beat egg in large bowl. Add evaporated milk, sage, salt and pepper. Mix. Add venison, cracker crumbs, 1/2 cup of cheese and soup mix.

Blend and form into loaf and place in 2-qt. pan. Lay bacon on top and sprinkle rest of cheese on top. Bake for 50 minutes.

William H. George, Jr.
Canton, Pennsylvania

Southern Fried Venison

3	lbs. venison steak
2	tsp. black pepper
1 1/2	cup flour
1/2	cup cooking oil
2	medium yellow onions, sliced
1	garlic clove, crushed
4	bouillon cubes or can of beef broth
	water
1	heaping T. Lipton's Onion Soup mix
2	heaping tsp. cornstarch

Mix black pepper and flour in shaker bag and coat steaks. Preheat oil in deep skillet. Brown both sides of steak. Remove from pan and set aside. Pour off excess oil. Return to pan and add onion, garlic, bouillon or broth, and enough water to cover by 1 inch. Add soup mix and stir. Add meat, then cover and simmer 1 to 1 1/2 hours or until tender. Remove venison and make gravy by mixing cornstarch with 1 cup cold water. Stir until desired thickness. Return steaks to gravy and serve.

William H. George, Jr.
Canton, Pennsylvania

Alabama Venison Stir-Fry

3   lbs venison tenderloin, cut into bite-sized
     pieces
1/4 cup vegetable oil
2   T. steak seasoning
5-6 large potatoes, peeled and cut into small
     pieces
1   small pkg. of carrots, cut into small pieces
1   onion, chopped
1/2 bell pepper, chopped
1   16-oz. can of corn
1   head of broccoli, cut into small pieces
1   small head of cauliflower, cut into small pieces
1   envelope, dry onion soup mix
     salt and pepper to taste

In a wok, add vegetable oil, then add the tenderloin,
and stir. Add seasoning, potatoes and carrots. Cook for
a few minutes, stirring occasionally. Add chopped
onion, bell pepper and cook for 10 minutes, or until
meat is brown. Add corn, broccoli, cauliflower and
onion soup mix. Cover and simmer for 10 minutes or
until broccoli and cauliflower are tender. Add salt and
pepper if desired. Serve hot with salad and garlic bread.

William E. Tyson, Jr.
Toxey, Alabama

Corned Venison

 5   lbs. venison, boneless
 4   cups hot water
 2   cups coarse salt
 1/4 cup sugar
 2   T. mixed whole pickling spice
 1 1/2 tsp. saltpeter
 3   garlic cloves

Bring above ingredients, except meat, to a boil. Cool.
Put boneless meat in large container. Pour cooled
mixture over meat. Add 3 garlic cloves if desired.
Weight the meat to keep it submerged.

Cure in refrigerator or a cool place for 3 weeks, turning
the meat every 5 days. To cook, wash meat under
running cold water, cover with boiling water and
simmer until done.

Welton Ernst
Lan Co., Nova Scotia, Canada

Venison with Peppers and Tomatoes

1 ½   lbs. sirloin steak, cut into
       1-inch thick cubes
  4   T. margarine or butter
  2   green peppers, cut into strips
  2   tomatoes, chopped
  1   tsp. dried oregano
  1   tsp. Worcestershire sauce
      salt to taste
 ½   tsp black pepper

Melt margarine in large skillet over medium heat.
Brown meat in margarine, remove, keep warm. Add
peppers, tomatoes, oregano, Worcestershire sauce, salt
and pepper.

Cook for 5 minutes or until peppers are softened.
Return meat to skillet. Cook for 2-3 minutes or until
steak is done.

Welton Ernst
Lan Co., Nova Scotia, Canada

Venison Stroganoff

1 1/2   lbs. venison round steak
1/4   cup butter
1   cup mushrooms, sliced
1   T. flour
1/2   cup sour cream
1   tsp. salt
1/2   tsp. pepper

Cut steak in 1-inch strips, 1/4-inch thick. Melt half the butter in a large covered skillet. Add venison and brown lightly on medium heat. Cover and stir occasionally, adding the mushrooms after 15 minutes. Cover and continue cooking on low heat for another 10 minutes. Set meat and mushrooms aside on a warm platter. Melt remaining butter in skillet on low heat, add flour and stir until smooth. Add sour cream and simmer until warm. Replace meat and mushrooms in skillet, season with salt and pepper, and stir until meat is coated with sauce. Heat thoroughly on low for 5 minutes; do not boil! Serve on platter of egg noodles with a side of garlic bread.

Dick Swihart
San Mateo, California

Dave's Venison Top

　 venison steaks, cut into bite-sized pieces
　 soy sauce
I 10³/₄-oz. can mushroom soup
I 2.8-oz. can French fried onions
　 instant mashed potatoes

Marinate venison in soy sauce for 30 minutes, turning once and adding more soy sauce. Brown venison with soy sauce. Add mushroom soup and French fried onions to meat. Mix together and heat. Serve over instant mashed potatoes

Dave O'Mara
La Crosse, Wisconsin

Nutrition Label
What it means

Cholesterol Free: Less than 2 milligrams of cholesterol and 2 grams (or less) of saturated fat per serving.

Venison Stew

1-2 lbs. venison stew meat, cut into 1-inch cubes
3 T. cooking oil
2 garlic cloves, chopped
1 cup seasoned flour
1 large onion, chopped
1 beef oxo cube
1 cup warm water
1 celery stalk, chopped

3 medium-sized chopped potatoes
2 large carrots, chopped
1 cup catsup

Seasoned flour:
1 cup flour
1 tsp. salt
1/2 tsp. pepper
Mix thoroughly

To reduce the gameness of the meat, soak overnight in a solution of salt and water. Moose, elk or caribou could be used. Pour oil into a large skillet or Dutch oven and heat oil on high heat. Add garlic and cook until garlic turns dark brown. Remove garlic from pan. Place the seasoned flour into a large plastic bag, add all the meat to the bag and shake until the meat is coated. Add the meat to the hot oil and cook until meat starts to brown.

Stir continuously to prevent meat from sticking. Add onion and cook for a few minutes. Dissolve oxo cube in a cup of warm water and add to meat. Stir thoroughly and bring to a boil. Turn stove down to simmer, cover and cook for 15 minutes, stirring often to prevent sticking. Add celery and cook for another 10 minutes. Add potatoes and carrots. Cover and cook until vegetables are almost done, then add catsup, stir and cook until the meat is tender. If stew is too thick, add 1 cup of water during cooking. Serve with rice, garlic bread or thick slices of sourdough bread.

Walter Kiliwnik
Elphinestone, Manitoba, Canada

Country Venison

1 1/2 lbs. flank steak
  1 onion, finely chopped
  1 T. parsley, finely chopped
 1/2 cup red wine
  1 T. Worcestershire sauce
 1/2 cup venison broth, or substitute beef broth
  1 T. cornstarch dissolved in 2 T. cold water

Score the steak with a sharp knife. Combine the onion and parsley and press mixture into the scored venison. Place the meat in a shallow dish. Add the wine and Worcestershire sauce. Allow the venison to marinate for 1 hour, longer if possible, turning the meat once. Remove the meat from the marinade and dry on paper towels.

Broil the venison for 5 minutes on each side. Place the marinade in a small saucepan. Add venison broth or beef broth and bring to a boil. Stir in the cornstarch dissolved in cold water and allow the mixture to thicken into a sauce. Serve the sauce over the venison steak.

Swiss Venison Steaks

2-4   venison steaks
      flour
  1   cup catsup
 1/2   cup water
 1/4   cup vinegar
  1   T. mustard
  1   T. Worcestershire sauce
  1   cup onion, chopped
  1   T. garlic (optional)
  1   can mushrooms (optional)
      hot sauce (optional)

Dip steaks in flour and brown in greased skillet. Remove and place in roasting pan. Mix remaining ingredients and pour over steaks. Bake covered at 350 degrees for 2 to 2 1/2 hours or until fork tender.

Mark Reaver
London, Ohio

Mike's Venison Stew

2-3   lbs. venison, cut into 1-inch cubes
1 1/2 cup French dressing
  2   carrots, cut into 1-inch pieces
  1   large onion, chopped
  1   small green pepper, chopped
  3   celery stalks, cut into 1-inch pieces
  1   16-oz. can whole tomatoes, mashed
  1   whole clove
  1   bay leaf
     salt and pepper to taste

Marinate cubed venison in French dressing for 12 hours in refrigerator. Drain off salad dressing and place venison in Crockpot. Stir in remaining ingredients. Cover and cook on low setting for 8 to 10 hours.

Nutrition Label
What it means

Low Cholesterol: Twenty milligrams of cholesterol (or less) and 2 grams of saturated fat (or less) per serving.

Crispy Fried Venison

1 1/2	lbs. venison
1	cup flour
1	T. garlic salt
1	T. onion salt
1	T. coarse ground pepper
	bacon drippings or vegetable oil

Use any cut of venison and slice across grain into thin
pieces (1/4-inch). Pat dry with paper towels. Combine
flour and spices in paper bag. Place meat in bag and
shake until well-coated.

Preheat bacon drippings or oil in nonstick pan.
Fry meat over medium heat until dark brown and
very crisp.

Drain on paper towels and serve.

Bill Nahrstedt
Avon Park, Florida

Roast Venison Barbecue

4-6 lbs. venison roast
1/2 tsp. salt
I tsp. black pepper
I tsp. thyme
I tsp. oregano
I 9-oz. bottle barbecue sauce
I 16-oz. bottle of beer
2-4 T. Tabasco sauce
I bottle Good Seasons Italian dressing
1/2 cup Worcestershire sauce

Place roast in Dutch oven. Rub salt, pepper, thyme and oregano into roast. Mix remaining ingredients and pour over roast. Cover roast with marinade for 8 hours or overnight. Cook roast (in Dutch oven) with marinade for 2-3 hours on grill or in oven at 350 degrees. Serve as roast or slice for hot roast venison sandwiches on fresh rolls.

Nutrition Label
What it means

Reduced Cholesterol: At least 25 percent less cholesterol than higher-cholesterol version, and 2 grams (or less) of saturated fat per serving.

Roast Crabapple Venison

5-6 lbs. venison roast, boneless
1/2 tsp. salt
I tsp. pepper
I garlic clove, crushed

Marinade:
1/4 cup orange juice
2 T. lemon juice
1/4 tsp. all spice

Glaze:
2 T. melted butter
2 T. orange juice
1/4 cup crabapple jelly

Season roast with salt, pepper and garlic. Tie roast with cooking twine and place in covered baking dish. Roast in preheated oven at 350 degrees for 1 to 1 1/2 hours. Combine 1/4 cup orange juice, lemon juice and allspice to form marinade and baste meat frequently. To make the glaze, mix melted butter, 2 T. orange juice and crabapple jelly in bowl. Thirty minutes before roast is done, uncover and brush meat with glaze and continue roasting until desired doneness.

Sauerbraten (Venison Style)

6	lbs. venison roast, boneless and cubed
I	cup sugar
2	cups water
3	cups vinegar
I	1/4-oz. can pickling spice
I	large onion, sliced
10-15	gingersnap cookies, crushed

Place roast in Dutch oven. Mix sugar, water, vinegar, pickling spice and onion. Pour mixture over roast. Marinate roast overnight or longer (the longer it marinates, the more tart it will taste). Cook slowly on top of stove for 1 1/2 hours. When done, pour juice through strainer to make gravy with crushed gingersnaps instead of flour. Serve on egg noodles or dumplings.

Nothing Artificial

Perhaps the biggest advantage of wild game over commercially raised cattle is that there are no artificial preservatives used in processing the game meat.

Dave's Chernobyl Chili

2	lbs. ground venison
I	8-oz. can V-8 juice
I	12-oz. bottle beer
I	large onion, chopped
I	4-oz. can green chilis, diced
I	14-oz. can tomatoes, diced
I	4-oz. can sliced mushrooms
I	4-oz. can jalapenos, diced
4	T. chili powder
I	T. garlic powder
I	T. cumin
I	T. oregano
I	T. pepper
I	tsp. paprika
I	tsp. celery salt
2	tsp. cayenne pepper
	salt to taste
I	16-oz. can kidney beans, drained

Brown meat with green chilis and onion. Drain off fat. In large saucepan, add all ingredients except kidney beans. Cover and let simmer for 1 hour, stirring occasionally. Add kidney beans during the last 10 minutes of cooking.

David Compton
Lakewood, California

Ron's Venison Jerky

2 lbs. venison, thinly sliced into strips
1/4 cup soy sauce
1 tsp. pepper
1 tsp. salt
1/4 tsp. garlic powder
1/2 tsp. onion powder
1 tsp. liquid smoke
3 dashes Worcestershire sauce
1/4 tsp. red pepper, crushed (optional)
1/4 tsp. meat tenderizer

Mix all ingredients (except meat) in large bowl. Soak meat in sauce for 1 hour. Hang meat in oven with toothpicks (put a drip pan under meat). Cook at 200 degrees for 5 hours. Leave oven door cracked open during cooking.

Ron Offerman
Channahon, Illinois

Venison Stove Top Stuffing Casserole

Stove Top stuffing for 6 people
I onion, sliced
I lb. ground venison (moose, elk, antelope)
    salt and pepper to taste
I can cream of mushroom soup
I can cream of chicken soup
I cup water

Fix Stove Top stuffing as directed on package. Mix onions with meat in skillet and cook until meat and onions are done. Add salt and pepper to taste. Mix mushroom soup, chicken soup and water together. Layer the meat mixture in bottom of casserole dish, top with stuffing mix. Pour soup and water mixture over the top. Cover and bake at 450 degrees for 1 hour. May be cooked in microwave on high for 20 minutes.

John H. Salisbury
Green River, Wyoming

Stag Sirloin

2 lbs. venison, aged sirloin

Sauce:

1/2 lb. onions, minced	1/2 tsp. salt
1/2 pint good red wine	fresh pepper
3 juniper berries	1 fl. oz. red wine
1 small branch rosemary	(or water)
1 small bay leaf	salt and pepper
2 cloves	4 soupspoons dried
oil	raisins

Meat must be at room temperature before cooking. Heat oven to 175 degrees, with the braising pan in the middle of the oven. Heat sauce on very low heat for 45 minutes in a covered pan. Crush all sauce ingredients through a strainer to obtain 1/4-pint of liquid. If there is less, add red wine. If there is more, heat on low to evaporate the extra.

Heat the oil in a skillet. Pat meat dry with a paper towel, then add salt and pepper. Brown the meat on all sides for 4-6 minutes, then lower the heat. Put meat in heated braising pan in the oven and bake for 30 to 60 minutes depending on the thickness of the meat. If the meat cannot be served immediately, lower temperature to 140 degrees to keep it warm for a maximum of 45 minutes. Cut and serve immediately.

Wipe the skillet clean with paper towels, add the wine (water), heat, evaporate half, strain and add to the sauce. Heat in a saucepan, add the raisins, salt and pepper, and serve.

Frank N. Vallotton
Morgas, Switzerland

Vaira's Venison Vegetable Soup

2   lbs. venison stew chunks, cut from the flanks or
    use neck bone
2   celery stalks, chopped
3   carrots, chopped
1   medium potato, diced
1   medium onion, chopped
1/2 cup uncooked rice or egg noodles
16 cups water
1   28-oz. can crushed tomatoes
1   29-oz. can tomato sauce
1   16-oz. can corn

Seasoning:
1   T. garlic powder
1   tsp. oregano
2   tsp. basil
1   T. parsley flakes

Use at least an 8-qt. pot and brown the venison
chunks or boil the neckbone. When meat is cooked,
add remaining ingredients. Allow to simmer for several
hours. Yields a lot of soup.

Barbara A. Vaira
Wilmington, Illinois

West Virginia Sweet and Sour Venison

I   lb. venison steak, cubed
I   sweet onion, chopped
I   tsp. butter
I   T. soy sauce
    black pepper
    salt
I   red sweet pepper, sliced
I   medium sweet green pepper, sliced
2" piece of chopped ginger root or 4 hard shakes
    of dried ginger
I   carrot, sliced, or one small can sliced carrots

Sauce:
I   shot cooking wine or sherry
2   T. water
2   tsp. orange or lemon juice
I   4-6 oz. can pineapple chunks
I   4-oz. can tomato paste
2   T. brown sugar
3   T. wine vinegar
2   T. cornstarch or arrowroot

Brown the cubed venison and chopped onion in a large frying pan with butter. While browning, season mixture with soy sauce, black pepper and salt to taste. When almost done browning, add the red and green peppers and the ginger; flavor with remaining soy sauce. Stir-fry lightly to soften peppers. After about 2 minutes, add the carrots, wine, water, juice, pineapple, tomato paste, sugar and vinegar. Stir mixture until thoroughly mixed. Add more water if required to create a thin gravy-like mixture around the meat. Simmer for 45 minutes, then stir in cornstarch to thicken. Serve over rice or noodles.

Ramsey Roast Venison

4-5   **lbs. venison roast**
  1/4   **cup soy sauce**
  1/4   **cup Worcestershire sauce**
  1/4   **cup corn syrup**
  2   **cups water**
  1   **T. ginger**
  1   **T. paprika**
  1   **T. garlic powder or minced garlic**
  1   **package onion soup mix**
  1   **T. creole seasoning**
  1/2   **cup olive oil**
  2   **T. flour or cornstarch**
      salt and pepper to taste

Mix soy sauce, Worcestershire sauce and corn syrup together, add ginger, paprika, garlic and creole seasoning. Mix well. Rub venison roast with the mixture, then brown on both sides in oil. In Crockpot or slow cooker, add remaining mixture, 2 cups of water, package of onion soup mix, and the roast. Cook on medium (simmer) for 5 hours. Remove roast and slice. Add 2 T. flour or cornstarch to drippings. Bring to boil until thick. Ladle over roast slices. Salt and pepper to taste.

Jay Ramsey
Dunlap, California

Buckaroo Skew

3   lbs. venison, cut into 1-inch cubes
2   cups onion, diced
2   T. garlic, crushed
1/2 cup fresh parsley, diced
1   T. capers
1   cup sherry wine (not cooking sherry)
    favorite skewer veggies
    bamboo skewers

Combine venison cubes, onion, garlic, fresh parsley, capers and sherry wine into plastic bag. Shake well and store in refrigerator overnight.

Skew with favorite vegetables and grill over hot barbecue grill, 4 minutes per side.

Jay Ramsey
Dunlap, California

Big Game

Antelope

Bear

Boar

Buffalo

Caribou

Elk

Feral Hog

Moose

Sheep

Antelope with Sauerkraut and Sour Cream

2 lbs. antelope cut in 1-inch cubes (deer or elk may also be used)
1 T. flour
1 tsp. salt
1 T. paprika
2 onions, finely chopped
1 garlic clove, minced
1 tsp. caraway seeds
1/2 cup dry white wine
1 large can (27-oz.) sauerkraut (drained)
1 cup sour cream

This recipe is best done in clay cooker. If using one, soak top and bottom for 30 minutes in water before cooking. Coat meat in flour, salt and paprika. Place in cooker. If using a covered ovenproof casserole, brown meat with flour, salt and paprika before starting. Stir in onions, garlic and caraway seeds. Pour in wine. Place covered cooker in cold oven. Set oven at 425 degrees. Bake until meat is tender (1 1/4 to 1 1/2 hours). Stir in sauerkraut and bake covered for 30 minutes. Stir in sour cream, bake covered just until hot (about 10 minutes). Garnish with parsley. Serve with noodles.

Trophy Antelope Chili

2¹/₂ lbs. ground antelope
  I can stewed tomatoes
  4 8 oz. or 2 15-oz. cans of tomato sauce
  I I-oz. pkg. mild chili seasonings
  I I-oz. pkg. hot chili seasonings
  I 15-oz. can dark red kidney beans, drained
  I 15-oz. can spicy chili beans
 ¹/₄ cup onion, chopped
 ¹/₄ cup green pepper, chopped

Brown antelope, drain completely. Add stewed tomatoes and tomato sauce. Stir in chili seasonings, mix well. Add remaining ingredients. Simmer for at least 1 hour, preferably longer. Stir frequently to avoid burning. Chili will be thick. If ground beef is substituted, add 2 to 2¹/₂ tablespoons of ground sage.

Nathan S. Gilbertson
Grandin, North Dakota

Antelope Stew

2-3	lbs. antelope stew meat, cut in 1-inch cubes
1/4	cup flour
1/2	tsp. salt
1/2	tsp. pepper
1 1/2	cups beef broth
1	tsp. Worcestershire sauce
1	garlic clove, minced
1	bay leaf
1	tsp. paprika
4-6	carrots, sliced
3-5	potatoes, diced
1	onion, chopped
1	celery stalk, sliced

Put meat in Crockpot. Mix flour, salt and pepper. Pour over meat, and coat meat with flour. Add remaining ingredients and stir to mix well. Cover and cook on low for 10-12 hours (on high heat, cook 4 to 6 hours). Stir stew thoroughly before serving.

Ronald Winter
Woodhaven, Michigan

Antelope Fried Steak

2-4 antelope steaks
1 cup flour
1 tsp. salt
1 tsp. pepper
1 cup bread crumbs
1 egg
1/4 cup milk
    oil

Combine flour, salt, pepper and bread crumbs. Mix egg and milk together, dip steak into egg mixture, then place in bread crumb mixture. Cover entire steak and press down. Place in skillet with hot oil on medium-high heat.

Fry for 5 minutes on each side to seal in juices, then fry for an additional 10-15 minutes on each side.

Ronald Winter
Woodhaven, Michigan

Antelope Meat Loaf

2-3 lbs. ground antelope
1/2 lb. ground veal
1/2 lb. ground pork
I egg, beaten with milk
1/8 cup milk
I envelope Lipton onion soup mix
I small onion, chopped fine
I green pepper, chopped fine
bread crumbs for topping (optional)
catsup for topping (optional)

Knead antelope, pork and veal together. Mix in beaten egg mixture. Add onion soup mix, onion and green pepper. Form loaf into pan, cook 1 hour at 350 degrees in preheated oven. Sprinkle bread crumbs and catsup on top.

Cook for additional 30-45 minutes.

Ronald Winter
Woodhaven, Michigan

Bear Bourguignon

2   lbs. bear meat, cut into cubes
I   T. oil
2   T. flour
    salt and pepper
3   garlic cloves, minced
I   tsp. thyme
I   bay leaf
I   can golden mushroom soup
2   cans beef consommé
I   envelope onion soup mix
    mushrooms, sliced
I   onion, chopped in medium pieces
2   celery stalks, chopped into medium pieces

Cook the meat in oil until brown. Add flour, keep mixing. Add salt, pepper, garlic, thyme, bay leaf and all soups. Cook at least one hour at low heat. Add mushrooms, onions, celery, and cook for 2 more hours. Remove bay leaf before serving. Serve on mashed potatoes. One cup red wine may be used, but then only use 1 can of consomme.

John Morissette
Reading, Pennsylvania

Boar in a Biscuit

1	lb. ground boar
1/2	cup barbecue sauce
1/4	cup onion, chopped
1-2	T. brown sugar
1	10-oz. can refrigerated biscuits
2	oz. (1/2 cup) shredded cheddar or American cheese

Heat oven to 400 degrees. Grease 10 muffin cups. Brown boar in large skillet; drain. Stir in barbecue sauce, onion and brown sugar. Cook for one minute to blend flavors, stirring constantly.

Separate dough into 10 biscuits. Place one biscuit in each greased muffin cup. Firmly press in bottom and up sides. Spoon approximately 1/4 cup of meat mixture into each biscuit-lined cup. Sprinkle each with cheese. Bake at 400 degrees for 10-12 minutes, or until edges of biscuits are golden brown. Cool for 1 minute; remove from pan.

Can be made ahead: prepare as above, cover and refrigerate for up to 2 hours. Bake as directed. Ground venison may be substituted for ground boar.

R. Keith Pope
Woodbridge, Virginia

Boar Chops with Peppers

        4   wild boar chops or cutlets
        2   T. olive oil
        I   small onion, finely chopped
        I   red bell pepper
        I   green bell pepper
        2   garlic cloves
            paprika
            fresh ground pepper
        2   T. pickled capers, chopped

Heat oil in large skillet, add onion and cook until transparent. Remove seeds from peppers and cut into 1/2-inch squares. Mince garlic cloves. Add peppers and garlic to onion, and cook for approximately 10 minutes or until peppers soften. Coat boar chops with paprika. Add fresh ground pepper. Push the peppers and onions to one side of the pan and add the chops (can also place chops on top of peppers and onions if desired). Add minced capers. Cook chops until done.

Keith Baker
Falls Church, Virginia

Buffalo Jerky

3	lbs. buffalo meat
1/2	cup soy sauce
1/2	cup Worcestershire sauce
2	tsp. seasoning salt
2	tsp. onion powder
2	tsp. garlic powder
1	tsp. black pepper
2	tsp. Accent
10	drops Tabasco sauce

Slice meat into 3/8-inch strips. Combine remaining ingredients, stir until spices have dissolved. Place meat into mix, covering meat completely with sauce. Marinate overnight, turning occasionally. Lay strips over oven rack or single rack on a cookie sheet.

Cook at 150 degrees for 6-8 hours. The longer it cooks, the crispier it becomes. Store in an airtight container.

(If a teriyaki taste is desired, use 1/4 cup of teriyaki sauce.)

Gebe's Caribou Chili

2	lbs. ground caribou
1	medium onion, chopped
1	medium green pepper
2	garlic cloves
1/2	envelope onion soup mix
3	T. chili powder
1	16-oz. can tomatoes
1	tsp. sugar
2	T. barbecue sauce
1	7-oz. can mushrooms
dash	red hot sauce

Brown meat, onion and pepper in a large pot. Stir in rest of ingredients. Cover and simmer on low heat for 1-2 hours.

Todd Gebert
Sheboygan, Wisconsin

Dried Herbs Versus Fresh

Dried herbs are more pungent than fresh so if you're substituting dried for fresh in a recipe, cut the amount by half.

Elk Loin Bearnaise

> 4   elk loin steaks, 1-inch thick
>   olive oil
>   garlic powder
>   black pepper
> 1/2 recipe Knorr Bearnaise Sauce Mix

Rub each side of steak with a small amount of olive oil and season with a little garlic powder and black pepper. Marinate the steaks for 1/2 hour before cooking. Prepare the Bearnaise sauce according to package directions.

Broil the steaks 4 minutes on the first side, then 3 minutes on the other (for medium-rare meat).

Spoon Bearnaise sauce over each steak and serve.

Terry Stevenson
Leadville, Colorado

Roast Elk Cooley

3 lbs. elk roast	8 thin slices Swiss cheese
3 T. butter	1/2 cup bread crumbs
8 thin slices ham	onion cheese sauce

This recipe is best done in a clay cooker. If using one, soak top and bottom of cooker in water for 30 minutes before using. Place roast, tied, in cooker. Dot with 1 T. butter. Place cooker in cold oven and bake at 425 degrees for 1 3/4 hours.

Make onion cheese sauce. Take roast from cooker and remove strings. Carefully make 8 cuts into the roast, cutting almost through. Spread cut surface with onion cheese sauce and place 1 slice each of ham and cheese in each cut. Secure roast with long skewers and replace in cooker. Spread remaining sauce over roast. Melt 2 T. butter, mix with bread crumbs and sprinkle over roast. Bake, uncovered, 20-30 minutes until crumbs are crisp and brown. Place roast on warm serving platter. Stir cooking liquid to form a smooth sauce. To serve, remove skewers, slice, apply sauce.

Onion Cheese Sauce:

1 medium onion	dash pepper
1/3 cup butter	1 cup milk
1/4 cup flour	1/3 cup chicken broth
dash salt	1/4 cup grated Swiss cheese
dash nutmeg	2 T. Parmesan cheese

Sauté onion in butter until soft. Stir in flour and spices, cook until bubbling. Remove from heat. Stir in milk and broth. Cook over medium heat, stirring constantly until mixture thickens. Lower heat and cook, stirring for 2 minutes. Add cheeses and stir until melted.

Smoked Feral Hog

1 **feral hog**
juice from a large jar of jalapenos

Take hams, hind quarters, ribs, and marinate overnight in jalapeno juice. Use your favorite seasoning rub. Double-wrap each piece separately in aluminum foil, making a boat so the juices will not escape. Build a good wood fire, using mesquite, pecan or other wood, and let burn to coals. Smoke the hog for 12-14 hours until meat is done — time depends on the size of the pit and weight of the meat.

Louis E. Wells
Dripping Springs, Texas

Nutrition Label
What it means

Sodium Free (No Sodium): Less than 5 milligrams of sodium per serving, and no sodium chloride (NaCl) in ingredients.

Hearty Moose Stew

3-4	lbs. moose, cubed
2¹/₂	qt. water
3	medium carrots, diced
1	celery stalk, diced
3	small onions, diced
5	medium potatoes, diced
	flour to thicken
1¹/₂	tsp. salt
¹/₈	tsp. pepper

Remove meat from bone. Cut in 1¹/₂-inch cubes and place in 5-qt. kettle or Dutch oven with water. Boil until tender. Remove meat from kettle.

Place vegetables in the hot liquid and cook until tender. Return meat to kettle. Thicken gravy by adding flour to mixture. Add salt and pepper. Turn temperature down to simmer.

Serve in bowls or over baking powder biscuits.

Herbed Moose Roast

1	3-lb. moose roast
3	T. vegetable oil
1/2	tsp. dried marjoram
1/2	tsp. dried basil
2	tsp. salt
1/2	tsp. pepper
1	garlic clove, very finely diced

Place oil in small dish and add spices and garlic. Let stand for 30 minutes. Brush roast thoroughly with oil mixture using pastry brush.

Roast covered in 350-degree oven, 25-30 minutes per pound. Uncover for the last 15 minutes.

Welton Ernst
Lan Co., Nova Scotia, Canada

Eliminating Fat, Gristle

When cooking a roast, be sure to remove all the fat and white tissue from the meat. In order to get all the fat and gristle from the inside of the roast, break the meat apart, remove all gristle and white tissue, then fold back together and tie the roast with string before cooking.

Stuffing a Moose Heart

I	moose heart
1/2	cup vinegar
I	cup bread
I	lemon rind
I	egg, well-beaten
I	onion, minced
4	bacon slices, minced
	parsley
	basil
	salt and pepper
	fat or suet for browning
	flour for coating
I	cup red wine
	kneaded butter

Soak the heart for 4 hours in 1/2 cup vinegar, adding just enough water to cover the meat; then trim off the fat and gristle. For stuffing, mix bread, lemon rind, egg, minced onion, four slices of minced bacon, parsley, basil, salt and pepper. Melt some fat or suet in a thick and fairly large saucepan. Flour heart, brown on all sides, add one cup of water and cook on low heat for 4 hours in a covered casserole. One half hour before cooking is over, add red wine. When done, remove heart, thicken sauce with kneaded butter and serve.

Stewed Moose

> moose meat cut into 1-inch cubes
> 1   can cream of mushroom soup
> 1   envelope onion soup mix
> 1   16-oz. can ginger ale

Place meat in roasting pan. Add mushroom soup, onion soup mix and ginger ale. Cover and bake for 2 hours or until tender. Serve with mashed potatoes and green peas. Works well with other game as well.

Pearl Janes
Musgravetown, Newfoundland, Canada

Storing Frozen Fatty Meat

Fatty meats such as bear and boar should not be stored in a freezer for more than six months.

Smothered Moose Steak

3   lbs. round moose steak, 2¹/₂-inches thick
3   T. butter
     salt and pepper
3   large onions
I   28-oz. can tomatoes

Sear moose steak in butter on one side in Dutch oven. Turn, sprinkle with salt and pepper. Put onions over meat and add tomatoes.

Bake for 2 hours at 350 degrees. (Dutch oven must be steam proof.) Serve with baked potatoes and tossed salad.

Welton Ernst
Lan Co., Nova Scotia, Canada

Parboil, Then Cook

Even if you have a relatively young goat, it is best to parboil the meat at least an hour before cooking. Soaking overnight in a saltwater solution will also increase tenderness and help to bring out the natural flavor of the meat.

McClary's 4-RAM Crockpot Chili

Marinade:

1/2	lb. Corsican Ram	olive oil
1/2	lb. Texas Dahl Ram	vinegar
1/2	lb. Mouflon Ram	soy sauce
1/2	lb. Hawaiian Black Ram	
	or 2 lbs of your favorite ram meat	

Combine 4 parts olive oil, 2 parts vinegar, 1 part soy sauce. Marinate meat separately in sealed plastic bag for 24 hours. Rinse meat in cold running water.

Chili:

	nonstick cooking spray	1	12-oz. can beer
1	large yellow onion, diced	3-4	T. chili powder
3	fresh jalapeno peppers	1/2	tsp. black pepper
	lemon pepper		salt
	garlic powder	2	T. cumin
	celery salt	1	10-oz. can pinto
2	10-oz. cans whole		beans
	tomatoes with no salt, low fat		

Spray Crockpot with nonstick cooking spray. Set pot on low heat. Cube meat, trim any fat. Dice onion and jalapenos. Heat 5-6 T. olive oil in skillet. Season meat to taste with lemon pepper, garlic powder and celery salt. Put meat and onions in skillet, brown over medium heat. Put 1 can of undrained tomatoes in Crockpot. Drain the second can of tomatoes, then place in Crockpot. Smash tomatoes with wooden spoon. Add beer. Add skillet contents to Crockpot. Add 3-4 heaping T. chili powder, 1/2 tsp. black pepper, pinch of salt, 2 T. cumin and jalapenos. Cook on low heat for at least 6-8 hours. Spoon off excess fat after 4 hours. An hour before eating, add pinto beans. Serve with sourdough or corn bread.

John McClary
Cypress, Texas

Slewgundy Ridge Stew

2 lbs. bear meat, cubed
1 tsp. black pepper
1 pinch of salt
2 large red potatoes, cubed
4 carrots, cut into 1-inch-size chunks
2 small onions, halved
1/2 cup white wine
3 12-oz. cans of baked beans
1 T. brown sugar

In large pot, cook bear meat, pepper, salt, potatoes, carrots, onions, and wine on low heat, covered, for 45 minutes. Stir 3 or 4 times while cooking. (Bear meat needs to be cooked to at least 137 degrees F.) After 45 minutes, drain juice while still hot. Add beans and continue to cook on low heat for 30 minutes. Add brown sugar and stir well. Cook for an additional 45 minutes on very low heat, stirring every 15 minutes, until done. Serve with hot buns.

Paul Doucett
Brentwood, New Hampshire

Wild Pepper Steaks in Whiskey Cream Sauce

1/2"	thick cuts of elk or antelope
	coarse ground black pepper
1/4	cup (1/2 stick) butter
	salt to taste
1	medium onion, finely minced
1/4	cup beef broth
1/4	cup whiskey
1/4	cup heavy cream

Press pepper firmly into meat. Heat large skillet over high heat to melt butter. Add meat — constantly agitating skillet; add salt and cook meat until desired degree of doneness is attained, turning once with tongs (to protect loss of juices).

Remove meat to warmed platter. Reduce heat to medium. Add onions to skillet and brown. Add broth and whiskey. Simmer for 1 minute. Add cream. Bring to boil, let thicken slightly. Serve cream/onion sauce over steaks.

Breakfast Burritos

¹/₂ lb. ground moose meat
¹/₂ cup green onion, chopped
 4 eggs
 2 T. powdered milk
¹/₂ tsp. salt
¹/₄ tsp. pepper
 2 T. butter or margarine sausage seasoning to taste
¹/₂ cup cheddar cheese, shredded
 8 flour tortillas
   salsa (if desired)

Combine ground meat and green onion in large skillet and cook thoroughly. Combine eggs, powdered milk, salt and pepper; beat well. Melt butter in skillet over medium heat; add egg mixture and cook, stirring often until eggs are firm but still moist. Add sausage mixture and cheese, stirring well. Spoon an equal amount of sausage/egg mixture into center of each warm tortilla, roll up and serve immediately with salsa. To warm tortilla, wrap tightly in foil and bake at 350 degrees for 15 minutes or on a camp stove or flat rock by campfire.

Salsa

 2 28-oz. cans tomatoes, drained
 I large onion, chopped
 I tsp. garlic, crushed
6-8 jalapeno peppers, stems removed, cut into 4-5 pieces
¹/₄ cup fresh cilantro
 2 T. lime juice
dash salt

Combine all ingredients, bring to boil, cook 5 minutes. Cool, then process in blender.

Bill Shipton
Las Cruces, New Mexico

Taco Casserole

2   lbs. big game burger
2   large onions, diced
1   clove garlic, diced
2   T. oil
2   cups whole tomatoes, chopped with juice
2-3   cups 4-oz. green chilis, diced
1 1/2   pkgs. 9-oz. corn tortillas
2   lbs. mozzarella cheese, grated (or cheese of your choice)

Cook burger, onions and garlic in oil until done. Stir in tomatoes and chilis. Simmer uncovered 20 minutes, stirring occasionally. Cut tortillas in quarters. In a 9x13 casserole, layer tortillas, meat sauce and cheese. Repeat layers, ending with cheese. Bake at 350 degrees for 20-25 minutes, or until bubbly and brown. Let stand for 10 minutes. Cut into wedges and serve.

M.C. Grimm
Silt, Colorado

Company Breakfast

1	lb. big game sausage
1	onion, diced
10	eggs or equivalent in egg beaters
1 1/4	cup milk
8-12	oz., Monterey Jack and mild cheddar cheeses, shredded and mixed
1	can mushrooms, diced

Cook sausage and onions thoroughly. Spray baking dish with cooking spray. Add sausage. Combine eggs and milk, pour over meat mixture. Refrigerate overnight. Add cheese and mushrooms. Bake at 375 degrees for 1 hour, or until set.

Cool, slice and serve. May be baked, frozen, then reheated.

M.C. Grimm
Silt, Colorado

**Nutrition Label
What it means**

Very Low Sodium: Thirty-five milligrams of sodium (or less) per serving.

Wetzel's Wild Game Roast

3	lbs. of roast
2	T. peanut oil
I	large yellow onion, peeled and coarsely chopped
I	12-oz. can mushrooms, drained
1/2	tsp. pepper, or to taste
2	bay leaves, torn in half
1/2	cup beef stock or bouillon
3	dill pickles, chopped
I	cup sour cream

Place the oil in a large heated pot. Flour and brown the roast, then add all the remaining ingredients, except the sour cream. Cover and simmer for 1 1/2 hours or until meat is very tender. Add the sour cream and simmer for an additional 1/2 hour. Remove meat from pan, slice and serve with the rich sauce on top.

Andrew J. Wetzel
Titusville, Florida

Wild Game Round Steak

- 1 lb. round steak
- 2 large onions, diced
- 1 cup celery, diced
- 6 T. cooking oil
  seasoned salt
  white vinegar

Soak steak for ½ hour in water with 1 T. salt and 6 T. white vinegar. Lightly sauté onions and celery in large frying pan. Season steak, place in frying pan and cover with onions and celery. Cover frying pan and cook on medium heat for 10 minutes.

Flip steak, top with onions and celery, cover and cook for an additional 10 minutes. When done, add water to thin the gravy, or if too thin, cook uncovered until gravy thickens. Serve with whipped potatoes.

Joseph F. Bagdal
Cincinnati, Ohio

Montana Meat Loaf

1	lb. big game burger, mixed with 10 percent suet
1/2	cup bread crumbs
1/2	cup milk
1	egg
1	T. onion, minced
1	T. American cheese, grated
1 1/2	T. steak sauce (A-1)
dash	Worcestershire, teriyaki and soy sauces
2	slices of bacon

Mix all ingredients except bacon and form into loaf.
Place in greased pan. Put bacon slices on top of loaf.

Bake at 350 degrees for 1 hour.

Clifford Gerrella
Billings, Montana

Beware Polar Bear Liver

If you ever have the opportunity to hunt
polar bear or at the least, eat the meat,
remember to never, ever eat the liver. Polar
bear liver is so high in vitamin A that it
can be lethal to humans.

All-Game Jerky

2 lbs. stripped game meat (or fowl breasts)
 1/4-inch thick
1 cup Worcestershire sauce
2 T. liquid smoke
2 T. onion powder
1 T. red pepper flakes (or more, to taste)
1 cup soy sauce
2 T. black pepper
2 T. garlic powder
2 tsp. brown sugar
 hot sauce to taste

Cut meat with the grain for chewy texture; cut across grain for crisp texture. Put meat in glass container with airtight lid. Mix all other ingredients and pour over meat. Marinate for at least 24 hours. For oven cooking, bake at 150 degrees for 12 to 16 hours, or until dried. In dehydrator, cook 24 to 36 hours or until dried. Sauce is enough for 4-5 pounds of meat.

Joseph Duckert
Arlington, Texas

Greek-Style Game Stew

3-3 1/2   **lbs. lean elk or antelope**
2   **lbs. small onions, peeled and quartered**
I   **cup olive oil**
1/2   **bulb garlic, peeled and separated**
1/2   **cup vinegar (wine or cider)**
I 1/2   **lbs. tomatoes (halved)**
2   **bay leaves**
I   **tsp. rosemary**
  peppercorns to taste
  water

Cut meat into 1-inch x 2-inch cubes. Put all the ingredients in cooking pot. Add water until everything is covered. Cover and place over medium-high heat.

After boiling, reduce heat to low and simmer for 2-3 hours. All the water/broth should be absorbed with only the oil remaining. Serve with a Greek salad and crusty bread.

Big Game Parmesan

    3   garlic cloves, diced fine
    1   large onion, chopped fine
   1/2 tsp. Italian seasoning
    1   1-lb. 14-oz. can whole tomatoes, chopped
        fine with juice
  1 1/2 lbs. roast or steak (frozen)
    3   eggs or equivalent in egg beaters
   1/2 cup milk
    1   cup unseasoned bread crumbs
   1/2 cup grated Parmesan cheese
   2-3 lbs. mozzarella cheese, sliced
        oil as needed

Sauté garlic, onions and seasonings until onions are clear. Add tomatoes and simmer for 30 minutes. Set aside and let cool. As meat thaws, slice as thinly as possible. Mix eggs and milk in a bowl. Mix bread crumbs and Parmesan cheese in a bowl. Dip slices of meat first in the egg and milk mixture, then in the bread crumbs and Parmesan. Fry until brown on each side (be careful not to lose the coating). In a 9x13 shallow dish, layer meat then cheese, then sauce. Sprinkle with grated Parmesan. Bake at 350 degrees or until cheese melts. Allow to set for 10-15 minutes. Slice and serve.

M.C. Grimm
Silt, Colorado

Wild Game Low-Fat Health Burgers

2½ lbs. ground game meat
⅓ cup Worcestershire sauce
⅔ cup gourmet sauce marinade
⅛ cup liquid smoke
¼ cup bran, wheat germ or multi-grain
2 egg whites
1 onion, chopped fine
2 T. Molly McButter
1 T. Mrs. Dash
   garlic powder (optional)

Remove all trimmings and fat, tendons and connective tissue from meat, so only red meat is left. Coarse-grind into burger. Mix all ingredients in a bowl. Form into patties. (Because they are low-fat, very little shrinkage will occur.) While cooking over the grill, sprinkle with Molly McButter and a touch of Mrs. Dash. A sprinkle of garlic powder can also be used.

Jeff Giddings
Anoka, Minnesota

Italian Game Loaf

1/2	lb. ground ground beef
1/2	lb. ground boar (or very lean ground pork)
1/2	cup bread crumbs
3	egg whites, lightly beaten
1/4	cup Romano cheese, shredded
1/4	T. thyme
1/4	T. nutmeg
1	T. oregano
2/3	cup tomato sauce
1	slice prosciutto
4	plum tomatoes
1 1/3	cups ricotta cheese
1/4	cup fresh parsley, minced
	black pepper

Preheat oven to 350 degrees. Mix meats, crumbs, egg whites, Romano cheese, herbs (except parsley) and tomato sauce. Coat loaf pan with grease or baking spray, press mixture into pan, and cut a deep V-shaped groove or trench into the top, lengthwise. Bake for 1 hour. Slice prosciutto, dice tomatoes and mince parsley. Mix with ricotta cheese. Remove loaf from oven and fill trench with ricotta mixture. Return to oven and bake for an additional 20 minutes. Let stand for 5 minutes before slicing. Serve with salad, pasta and bread.

Keith Baker
Falls Church, Virginia

Big Game Bean Stew

2	qts. pinto beans, cooked
1 1/2	lbs. ground game meat
1	onion, diced
1	tsp. salt
1/2	tsp. black pepper

Boil pinto beans in small pressure cooker or Crockpot. Brown ground meat and onion in skillet. Add salt and black pepper to meat. Mix bean and meat mixture and simmer for 1 hour.

John H. Salisbury
Green River, Wyoming

**Nutrition Label
What it means**

Reduced or Less Sodium: At least 25 percent less sodium per serving than the higher-sodium version.

Upland Birds

Crow
Dove
Chukar
Grouse
Partridge
Pheasants
Prairie Chicken
Quail
Sage Chicken
Turkey

Skillet Crow

8-10 crow breasts
       salt and pepper to taste
 2 T. butter
 1 1/2 cup sherry or white wine
 3 T. heavy cream

Sprinkle crow breasts with salt and pepper. Melt butter
in heavy cast-iron skillet. Brown breasts on both sides
for about 5 minutes each side. Add sherry or white
wine and simmer covered until tender. Cooking time
depends on age of crows; test with a fork.

Arrange breasts on a serving platter. Skim any fat from
the skillet sauce, and heat to a gentle boil, stirring with
a fork. Slowly stir in heavy cream and pour over
breasts before serving. Serve with rice.

Ronald M. Tussel, Jr.
Hawley, Pennsylvania

Dove with Pineapple

10   dove breasts, sliced into 20 fillets
2   oz. (¹/4 cup) Worcestershire sauce
10   pineapple chunks
10   slices of bacon

Dip each dove breast into Worcestershire sauce. Place chunk of pineapple between 2 fillets, wrap with bacon and secure with toothpick. Cook over charcoal fire until done (approximately 10 minutes). Serve as appetizer or as main dish over wild rice.

Terry M. Boyer
Lubbock, Texas

Closed Cavity Holds Moisture

Regardless of a game bird's size, the body cavity should always be closed before baking to hold in as much moisture as possible.

Dove Breast Teriyaki

10-20 dove breasts
teriyaki baste and glaze or
teriyaki with honey and pineapple

Cut meat from breastbone of doves; baste meat with either of the teriyaki sauces and cook in butter on stove top for 1 to 2 minutes per side.

Bill Milligan
Yucca Valley, California

Storing Small Birds, Animals

Small, lean birds including vegetarian waterfowl can be safely stored in a freezer for six to nine months. Small game animals should be stored no more than one year in the freezer.

Peoria Dove Breasts

6   dove breasts
I   can golden mushroom soup
3-4   cups cooked rice

Precook dove breasts in microwave for 3 minutes.
Place breasts in casserole and cover with 1 can undilut-
ed golden mushroom soup. Cover with 3 or 4 cups of
cooked rice. Bake in oven at 325 degrees for 1 hour.

Oscar and Joan Weber
Peoria, Illinois

Removal Eases Objections

If you have friends that are a little uneasy
about eating wild game meat, here's a
suggestion that could make your next
get-together with them a success. As we all
know, game meat doesn't taste bad, it just
tastes different. Before serving to the table,
especially for game birds, remove all bones
from the meat. This way the sight of the
unusual sized bones won't be a reminder to
your guests, and they will concentrate on the
flavor of your meal rather than the differ-
ences between game and "regular" meat.

Chukar a la Orange

I chukar, cut up
   teriyaki sauce
   salt and pepper to taste
   onion slices
   orange slices
I garlic clove, sliced
2 pieces bacon

Place chukar pieces on a large piece of aluminum foil. Sprinkle with teriyaki sauce, salt and pepper. Separate onion slices into rings and place on chukar pieces. Place orange slices on top. Add garlic and top with bacon. Loosely seal the foil packet. Place on a covered charcoal grill and bake for 1 hour, using indirect heat.

Recipe also works well with pheasant.

David Runde
Teutopolis, Illinois

Appetizing Chukar

2	chukar, deboned
1/4	tsp. garlic salt
1/4	tsp. pepper
1	T. Worcestershire sauce
2	green onions, finely chopped
1	dash red or white wine
4	large mushrooms, finely chopped
1/2	cup grated sharp or mild cheddar cheese
	crackers

Cut chukar into 1/4-inch or 1/2-inch pieces. Add next 5 ingredients to chukar. Marinate for at least 6 hours. Fry meat quickly until browned and just done. Add mushrooms and cook, stirring until heated through. Sprinkle with cheese, stir until melted. Serve hot on crackers. Makes about 2 dozen appetizers. Add spices to taste. Also works well with duck and quail.

Melissa Small
Reno, Nevada

Garlic Grouse

1-2   grouse
       butter
  4   garlic cloves, sliced

Remove all the meat from the birds. Cut the meat from breast, legs and wings into small pieces or strips. Heat butter in a frying pan, add garlic. When garlic has turned slightly brown, add meat. When edges start to brown and get a little crisp, the meat is done.

Ed Anderson
Campbell Ford, Ontario, Canada

**Nutrition Label
What it means**

Low Sodium: There can be 140 milligrams
of sodium (or less) per serving.

Dutch Oven Grouse

2   medium grouse
1/4 cup oil
salt and pepper to taste

Preheat oven. Cut the birds into serving pieces, and place in 12-inch Dutch oven, with 1/4 cup oil. Salt and pepper to taste. Cook very slowly for 1 hour.

Monte Bowthorpe
Moab, Utah

Eating Crow

Crows were once commonly eaten in this country, but no longer. However, if you'd like to try crow or have the opportunity, the meat can be a little tough if not properly prepared. Parboiling for at least an hour before cooking is recommended. If your crow is young, it might be more tender and juicy. Generally, you can substitute crow for any of the small game birds in your favorite recipes.

Lemon Grouse

4	boned, skinned and separated grouse breasts
1/4	tsp. gourment powder or **M.S.G.**
	dash pepper
1/4	tsp. salt
1	T. light soy sauce
1	cup flour
1/2	tsp. baking powder
1	egg, beaten with dash of salt
1	cup water

Lemon Sauce:

1	T. tapioca starch
3/4	cup water
1	T. white vinegar
3	T. white sugar
1/4	tsp. lemon extract
6-8	slices fresh lemon
	drops yellow food color (optional)

Marinate grouse breasts with gourmet powder, pepper, salt, light soy sauce for 1/2-1 hour. Prepare batter mix with flour, baking powder, egg and water. Dip grouse into the mixture and deep fry at 400 degrees for 5-10 minutes until golden brown. While waiting for the grouse to be cooked, use a saucepan to prepare the lemon sauce with starch, water, vinegar, sugar, lemon extract and fresh lemon slices. Cook over medium heat until boiled, keep stirring while cooking. For a golden color, add a few drops of yellow food coloring. Chop grouse into bite-sized pieces. Pour lemon sauce on top and serve hot.

Darlene Clark
Port Alberni, British Columbia, Canada

Maine Guide Grouse

 4   partridge breasts, cut into 1-inch cubes
 1   small onion, chopped
 1/2 dozen mushrooms, sliced
 2   T. butter
     garlic salt to taste
     black pepper to taste
 1/4 cup light beer

Lightly brown the onions and mushrooms with the butter in a deep skillet. Add the partridge, garlic salt, pepper and beer (do not exceed 1/4 cup).

Cook over medium heat (open-flame campfire), stirring occasionally until done. This will be very tender.

Serve with rice and asparagus.

Paul Doucett
Brentwood, New Hampshire

Stuff Bird Properly

If you're going to stuff your bird for cooking, and this applies to any bird you're going to cook, stuff it right before you're going to put it in the oven. Before stuffing let the dressing cool completely. Warm stuffing will increase the likelihood of bacterial growth in the bird's cavity.

Fried Partridge

I	**partridge**
1/4	**cup flour**
1/2	**tsp. paprika**
I	**tsp. salt**
1/4	**tsp. pepper**
4	**T. fat**
I	**cup milk**
	cooking sherry (optional)

Cut partridge into serving pieces. Dredge in flour, paprika, salt and pepper. Fry in hot fat until golden brown. Lower heat, cover tightly and let steam until tender.

Remove from pan and warm while making gravy. Add 1-2 tablespoons flour to fat in pan, slowly add milk and stir until thick. Add a little cooking sherry for a nice flavor.

Welton Ernst
Lan Co., Nova Scotia, Canada

Baked Pheasants in Cream Sauce

- 2 pheasants
- I can of milk
- 3/4 cup flour
- 2 cans cream of mushroom soup
- I can of mushrooms
    salt and pepper to taste

Preheat oven to 275° for 15 minutes. Spray 9 x 13-inch pan with nonstick cooking spray. Rinse the pheasants and clean the cavities well. Remove any excess fat. Cut the pheasants into halves and dip the halves in a bowl of the canned milk. Roll halves in flour, place halves in pan and bake for 30 minutes. Pheasant meat is very lean, so after 15 minutes of baking, check and see if the birds are cooked through. (The juices should run clear when the thickest part of the thigh is tested with the tip of a knife.) Mix leftover milk, flour, 2 cans of soup and 1 can mushrooms. Add 2-percent or whole milk to thin mixture to gravy thickness. Pour over pheasants. Raise temperature to 375 degrees. Bake for 1 hour, or until bubbly and golden brown. Serve with gravy poured over rice.

Mike McCabe
Rigby, Idaho

Pan-Roasted Pheasant

- **4** pheasant breasts, boned (or equivalent other bird)
- **3** garlic cloves, crushed
- **6** T. fresh lemon juice
- **6** T. Worcestershire sauce
- **1/2** cup water
- **4** T. melted butter
  cayenne pepper to taste
  black pepper to taste
- **1/3** cup fresh parsley, minced

Preheat oven to 375 degrees. Use a medium-size glass or enamel baking pan (don't use metal). Mix garlic, lemon juice and Worcestershire sauce with 1/2 cup water. Add the butter, black and cayenne pepper and half the parsley. Cross-hatch the top of each breast with 4 cuts, each about 1/4-inch deep. Place breasts, scored side down, and spoon sauce over the top side to coat. Bake breasts, uncovered, for 20 minutes (a little less for quail). Remove from oven and stir remaining parsley into sauce. Serve breasts scored-side up and pour a spoonful of sauce on top.

D.K. Baker
Falls Church, Virginia

Pheasant Adele

2   pheasant breasts, boned
I   small tomato, chopped
I   ripe avocado, chopped
2   oz. Monterey Jack cheese with jalapeno
    peppers
    parsley sprigs, chopped
I   garlic clove
    olive oil
    paprika
    black pepper

Preheat oven to 400 degrees. Chop tomato, avocado and cheese into small chunks. Coarsely cut up fresh parsley. Pound the pheasant breasts flat, to about 1/4-inch thick. Fill with tomato, avocado, cheese, parsley mixture, form a pocket and close with skewers. Cut garlic clove in half, score with a knife and rub the surface areas of the pheasant. Then brush olive oil over the exposed surface. Finally, cover pheasants liberally with paprika and fresh ground black pepper. Place in a baking pan and bake for about 40 minutes. Check midway and, if the pheasants appear to be too dry, brush again with olive oil. You can also add ham, pine nuts or raisins.

D.K. Baker
Falls Church, Virginia

Pheasant

2   whole pheasant breasts, deboned and skinned
    salt
    white pepper
    flour
1   egg with 1 tsp. water, whisked
2   cups fine bread crumbs
4   T. olive oil
    butter
2   cups white game sauce

Slice each breast into 2 equal-sized pieces. Season each piece with salt and white pepper. Roll them in flour, dip in egg wash, and coat with bread crumbs. Cover and refrigerate for several hours. To cook, pour olive oil and a small pat of butter in a preheated cast-iron skillet. When the oil is hot, saute the pieces for 2-3 minutes per side. Turn frequently until golden brown. Remove and drain. Serve with seasoned white sauce.

White Game Sauce:

1   T. butter   white pepper
1 1/2   T. flour   chicken bouillon to taste
2   cups chicken stock

Melt the butter in a saucepan over medium heat. Add the flour and cook 3-4 minutes, whisking often. Remove from heat and let cool slightly. Add the chicken stock, return to the stove over low heat, whisking until the liquid thickens and becomes shiny. Season to taste with white pepper and chicken bouillon.

Richard A. VonFeldt
Larned, Kansas

Marinated Pheasant Breast

5	lbs. pheasant breasts
1/3	cup apple cider vinegar
1/3	cup vegetable oil
1	tsp. onion salt
2	tsp. garlic powder
1	tsp. sweet basil
1	T. dried mint leaves or 5-7 fresh leaves
1	T. crushed rosemary
1	T. dried parsley or 1 fresh sprig
1	tsp. celery salt
1	dried bay leaf, crushed
1	tsp. salt
1/2	tsp. pepper

Combine all ingredients (except meat) and mix well. In a large sealable plastic bag or covered bowl combine meat and marinade and refrigerate for 2-3 days. Shake or stir 4 to 5 times while marinating. Grill breasts on low heat for approximately 1 hour and baste with remaining marinade during grilling.

Allen Faust, Jr.
Auburn, Pennsylvania

Pheasant with Peppers

   2   **pheasant breasts, boneless and skinless**
       paprika
   1   **red bell pepper**
   1/4 **lb. Portobello mushrooms**
   2   **garlic cloves**
   2   **T. olive oil**
       fresh ground pepper to taste

Cut pheasant breasts into strips and sprinkle generously with paprika. Remove seeds from pepper and julienne (cut into strips). Slice mushrooms. Crush garlic into skillet and add olive oil and peppers.

Heat over high flame until garlic is sizzling. Add ground pepper and stir-fry until pheasant is done. Serve immediately.

Keith Baker
Falls Church, Virginia

Elegant Pheasant Breasts

8   pheasant breast fillets
8   bacon slices
4   oz. dried beef
I   can cream of mushroom soup
I   can sour cream
    paprika to taste

Wrap each pheasant breast with a slice of bacon. Cover bottom of greased 9x13-inch pan with dried beef. Arrange pheasant breasts on top.

Blend soup and sour cream and pour over pheasant. Sprinkle each with paprika.

Bake uncovered for 2 hours at 300 degrees.

Jacki Moellenberndt
Fairbury, Nebraska

Creamy Pheasant Breast

1	pheasant breast, deboned flour seasoned with pepper
2	T. butter
2	T. cooking oil
1	11-oz. can cream of mushroom soup
1/2	can milk
1/4	tsp. rosemary, crushed cooked pasta (medium-wide egg noodles) parsley sprigs

Flour breasts and lightly brown in the butter and oil in a heavy skillet over medium-high heat. Mix soup, milk and rosemary. Pour over breasts. Bring to boil.

Cover, reduce heat and simmer for 1 to 1 1/2 hours (older birds take longer). Add milk or water if the sauce gets too thick.

Spoon over the cooked pasta and garnish with parsley.

Rodney Grimes
Dayton, Ohio

Southwest Pheasant

6-8	pheasant breasts, halved, skinned and boned
2-3	tsp. ground cumin
1 1/2	tsp. garlic salt
1-2	T. olive oil
1-2	cups black or pinto beans, rinsed and drained
1	8-oz. can or frozen kernel corn
1	cup picante sauce
1/2-2/3	cup red bell pepper, diced
2-3	T. cilantro, chopped

Sprinkle both sides of pheasant with half the cumin and half the garlic salt. Heat oil in skillet over medium heat. Add pheasant; cook for 3-4 minutes. In medium bowl, combine beans, corn, picante sauce, red pepper and remaining cumin. Turn pheasant; spoon bean mixture evenly over pheasant. Reduce heat to medium. Cook uncovered for 6-7 minutes or until pheasant is cooked through. Push bean mixture off pheasant into skillet. Transfer pheasant to serving platter, using slotted spoon; keep warm. Cook bean mixture over high heat 2-3 minutes or until thickened, stirring frequently. Spoon over pheasant. Sprinkle with cilantro and serve with additional picante sauce.

Serve with salad and cornbread or tortillas.

Pheasant Fajitas

2	pheasants, cut into bite-sized pieces
I	onion, sliced
I	green pepper, diced
I	envelope taco seasoning
1/2	cup water
	salt and pepper to taste
	flour tortillas
	cheddar cheese, shredded
	salsa
	sour cream

In large skillet, add pheasant, onion, pepper, taco seasoning and water. Simmer until meat is done (about 15 minutes). Drain. Spoon meat mixture onto tortillas, add cheese, salsa and sour cream.

Steve Taylor
Edwardsville, Kansas

Sprinkle, Wash

Another way to eliminate the "gamey" taste in birds is to sprinkle the body cavity with salt and pepper, then wash out with vegetable oil mixed with lemon juice. Before roasting, put a teaspoon of jelly inside.

Fried Pheasant with Rice

1	pheasant, cut into serving pieces
2	cups flour
1	tsp. salt
1/4	tsp. pepper
1/4	tsp. paprika
1/4	cup shortening
1 1/2	cups water
1	cup instant rice

Dress pheasant and cut into serving pieces. Mix flour, salt, pepper and paprika in plastic bag. Shake pieces of cut-up pheasant in bag until all are thoroughly coated with flour mixture. Melt shortening in large covered skillet. Brown pieces on all sides at medium/high temperature. Cover skillet, add 1/2 cup water, lower temperature and continue to simmer pheasant for another 1/2 hour. Add remaining water and rice, replace cover and steam for 15 minutes. Recipe works well using either young or old birds.

Dick Swihart
San Mateo, California

Pheasant and Potatoes

I	pheasant, skin removed, cut into pieces
1/2	tsp. garlic powder
1/2	cup onion
4	potatoes, quartered
I	cup stewed tomatoes
1/2	cup white wine
1/4	tsp. oregano
I	T. basil
	salt and pepper to taste

Brown pheasant pieces on all sides in frying pan or broiler. Place in a baking pan. Sprinkle with garlic powder. Place onions and potatoes in the pan. Combine remaining ingredients and pour over pheasant and potatoes. Bake at 350 degrees for 1 hour covered with aluminum foil, or until pheasant is tender. Bake uncovered for another 20 minutes.

Kenneth W. Crummett
Sugar Grove, West Virginia

Happy Pheasant

 4+   pheasant breasts, defatted and skinned
       flour
       cooking oil
       salt and pepper
 2-3   small onions
       green peppers
       mushrooms
1 1/2-2 cups sauterne wine (or other white wine)

Roll pheasant breasts in flour. Place in frying pan with
oil, cook until light brown on both sides. Salt and pepper to taste while in pan. When browned, remove
breasts from pan and place in a roaster. Add onions,
green peppers and mushrooms to leftover oil in pan
and saute until soft. Pour mushroom mixture over
pheasants in roaster. Add wine. Place in oven and bake
(uncovered) at 375 degrees for 30-35 minutes. Also
works with grouse, dove or chicken.

Michael F. Sestak
Erie, Pennsylvania

Crockpot Prairie Chicken

2	prairie chickens, boned
I	large onion, diced
	flour
	salt and pepper
¹/₂	cup celery, chopped
I	cup carrots, chopped
4-5	potatoes, sliced
I	can cream of mushroom soup
I	can cream of chicken soup
I	can Rotel tomatoes
I	15-oz. can tomato sauce

Spread onion on bottom of Crockpot. Coat chicken with flour and salt and pepper. Place meat over onion. Layer vegetables, then soup, tomatoes and sauce. Cook on low heat for 8 to 10 hours. Stir and serve over biscuits or bread. (Recipe also works with doves.)

Steve Taylor
Edwardsville, Kansas

Quail and Wild Rice

15 cleaned quail
 2 boxes of wild rice
 1 can of mushrooms or 1 cup of fresh, sauted
1/2 cup of almond halves or pecans
 1 cup of red wine (Lambrusco)

Cook wild rice according to directions on box. Add mushrooms and almonds. Put rice in roasting pan. Add quail and cover. Cook for 1 hour at 275 degrees or until tender. Halfway through cooking time, stir in wine, then re-cover.

Christine Thompson
Odin, Illinois

Check Bird's Sides

It's a good idea to check both breasts of a game bird if you're using juice release to determine how well done the bird is because the amount of shot that has entered the bird affects how much juice will escape. Naturally, you can only shoot the bird on one side or the other, so check both breasts to get a better idea of how done the bird is.

Mountain Quail or Chukar

7-8 full quail or 2-3 chukar
  2 cans cream of mushroom soup
  I cup sherry
  I cup sour cream
  I medium can mushrooms
    pinch salt
    pepper
    paprika
    basil
    oregano

Combine all ingredients in baking dish. Place quail or chukar in mixture and cover. Heat oven to 350 degrees. Bake for 1 hour. Serve over rice.

Bill Milligan
Yucca Valley, California

Drier Than Chicken

Pheasant meat is very similar to chicken, but is much drier. Therefore, you need to use every safeguard to ensure that maximum moisture is retained. Frequent basting helps. Since pheasant meat contains only about 5 percent fat, it is better suited to very moist cooking methods.

Big Bomber Sage Chickens

2	sage chickens
2	T. black pepper
2	T. white pepper
2	T. red coarse pepper
2	cups sifted flour
2-3	strips of bacon
2	T. sour cream

Bone and fillet 2 sage chickens. Combine peppers with flour. Coat chicken and brown. Layer chicken with bacon and sour cream. Bake for 2 hours at 350 degrees.

Mrs. Lonny Jennings
Point of Rocks, Wyoming

Potatoes Are Better

If your bird is likely to be too "gamey" tasting for you, don't stuff the body cavity with dressing. Instead, fill the cavity with peeled, cut-up raw potatoes, which will absorb flavor. Discard the spuds after the bird is cooked.

Better Than Mom's Turkey

1	14-lb. turkey
2	tsp. pepper
1/2	tsp. chili powder
1/2	tsp. ground sage
1/2	T. salt
1/2	T. seasoning salt
1/4	tsp. ground mustard
1/2	T. poultry seasoning
1 1/2	tsp. onion powder
1	tsp. garlic salt
1/4	cup brown sugar
4	T. butter
1/3	cup honey
1/3	cup Worcestershire sauce

Combine all dry ingredients in a bowl. In a microwavable bowl, combine butter, honey and Worcestershire sauce. Microwave until the 3 ingredients are heated and blended. Add to the dry mixture and stir well. Baste the inside and outside of the turkey with the mixture. Add remaining mixture to a full water pan for smoker. Smoke turkey, using a handful of hickory chips. Smoke until internal temperature of bird reaches 180 degrees. Use juices remaining in water pan to make gravy.

Herb Freeman
Logan, Utah

Wild Bird and Dressing "While You Work"

2-3   lbs. wild turkey or pheasant pieces
** 2   pkgs. Stove Top stuffing mix**
**   or packaged stuffing mix**
**   celery, chopped**
**   onion, chopped**

Spray large Crockpot with nonstick cooking spray.
Place pieces of turkey or pheasant on bottom of pot.
Prepare Stove Top stuffing or packaged stuffing mix
according to package directions, add onion and celery,
then cover meat.

Cook on low for 6-8 hours. If not completely cooked,
turn to high for 1-2 hours.

Frozen Large Game Birds

Large birds, both upland and fish-eating
waterfowl, should not be kept in a freezer
for more than six months.

Jacko's Wild Turkey

8-10	lbs. wild turkey
	salt and pepper to taste
1/2	lb. sausage meat
1/2	cup yellow onion, chopped
1	cup celery, chopped
1/2	tsp. thyme, crushed
1/4	cup parsley, chopped
1	cup cooked chestnuts, chopped
8	cups soft white bread, sliced into cubes
1	tsp. paprika
1	tsp. salt
4-6	slices bacon
5	juniper berries, crushed
	melted bacon fat (juices from bacon)
1	stick of butter

Sprinkle turkey inside and out with salt and pepper. Cook sausage meat in skillet until well done. Add onion and celery to skillet. Continue to cook until onion and celery are tender. Add thyme, parsley, chest-nuts, bread cubes, paprika and a tsp. of salt to skillet, mixing all ingredients well. Remove skillet from heat and spoon the mixture lightly into the neck and body cavities. Fry bacon in skillet until bacon is slightly cooked. Remove bacon and with toothpicks, pin bacon slices to the turkey's breast. Place turkey in roasting pan and put into a 400-degree oven (uncovered) until turkey turns brown. Now cover turkey with aluminum foil and lower oven temperature to 350 degrees. Cook turkey until tender, basting every 15 minutes, with the bacon fat and butter. Cooking time 1 to 1 1/2 hours.

M.A. Jacko
No. Versailles, Pennsylvania

Waterfowl

Coots
Ducks
Geese
Mud Hens

Barbecued Mallards or Coots

- 4 mallards or coots, dressed
- I tsp. basil
- I tsp. salt
- 1/4 tsp. fresh ground pepper
- I cup orange marmalade
- 1/2 cup orange juice
- I T. soy sauce
  cornstarch
  water

Broil ducks or coots on rotisserie for 50 minutes to 1 hour. Combine remaining ingredients except cornstarch in a saucepan. Bring to a boil. Make a thin paste of cornstarch and water. Gradually add to orange mixture, stirring continuously. Cook until mixture coats a spoon. Baste birds with sauce 3 times during the last 30 minutes of cooking time.

King's Coots

- 8 coot breasts
  Italian dressing
- I cup hot oil
  salt and pepper

Remove the breasts from coots, wash and place in bowl. Pour Italian dressing over breasts until covered. Refrigerate overnight. Heat oil in iron skillet. Drain coot breasts, salt and pepper to taste, then drop in skillet. Cook until brown and tender. Serve with biscuits and homemade cane syrup.

Lloyd King
Liberty, Mississippi

Cranberry Duck

1   mallard, canvasback or small goose

Stuffing:

1   apple, cored and chopped
1/2   cup celery, chopped

1   T. lemon juice
1   medium onion, chopped

Toss chopped apple with lemon juice to prevent pieces from turning brown. Add celery and onion.

Cranberry sauce:

2   cups water
1 1/2   cups whole cranberries, frozen or canned
1   cup applesauce

4   T. sugar
1/4   tsp. dry mustard
1 1/2   tsp. dry tarragon
1/2   tsp. salt, to taste

Heat oven to 350 degrees. Mix stuffing and stuff into bird until cavity is about 3/4 full. Place duck in roasting pan and cook for 45 minutes. While duck is cooking, prepare cranberry sauce. Bring water to boil and add cranberries, apple and sugar. Once soft, mash with a potato masher. Add remaining ingredients. Reduce heat and simmer for 10-15 minutes to blend flavors.

After the duck has been baked for 45 minutes, remove from oven and drain off any fat. Return duck to roasting pan and cover with half of the cranberry sauce. Cook another 45 minutes, occasionally basting with the remaining cranberry sauce.

Jim Preston
Winnipeg, Manitoba, Canada

Cranberry Duck Soup

leftover **Cranberry Duck, including all the
stuffing, leftover gravy and wild rice.**
2   **medium potatoes, diced (skin on)**
1   **medium onion, chopped**
2-3 **carrots, chopped**
4-6 **cups water (approximately)**
1/2 **cup cranberry if a little short of gravy, or you
want more cranberry flavor.
salt
Tabasco or Worcestershire sauce to taste
leftover wild rice**

Break up duck carcass and drop into large pot, along
with stuffing. Add enough water to cover. Simmer for
1-2 hours, adding water as needed. Remove from heat
and cool. Skim congealed fat off duck stock. Remove
meat from bones and return meat to pot. Add potatoes, onion, carrots, remaining gravy and cranberries.
Simmer soup until vegetables are almost tender. Add
salt, pepper, garlic, Tabasco, Worcestershire sauce, etc.
Add any leftover wild rice. The wild rice should not be
cooked too long as it tends to break up and cloud the
soup. Serve with garlic cheese toast.

Jim Preston
Winnipeg, Manitoba, Canada

Delta Duck a la St. Therese

- 8 duck breast halves (4 ducks)
  buttermilk
- 3 T. margarine
- I bay leaf
  garlic, minced
- I medium onion, finely chopped
- 5 sweet pickled onions
- 1/2 cup Madeira wine
- 1/2 lb. fresh mushrooms, sliced
  fresh parsley sprigs, chopped

Soak duck breasts overnight in buttermilk. Preheat oven to 325 degrees. Rinse breasts with water and pat dry. Melt margarine in fry pan. Sear breast fillets on each side quickly. Place in 3-qt. casserole, add bay leaf. In frying pan, saute garlic, onion and pickled onions; add wine and pour over ducks. Add salt and pepper.

Cover and bake 1 1/2 hours. Just before serving, saute mushrooms and a few sprigs of chopped parsley; use as garnish on ducks.

Duck Soup

- **4** ducks, cleaned
- **I** medium onion, chopped
- **2** potatoes, cubed
- **I** carrot, sliced
- **I** celery stalk, sliced and other vegetables preferred
- **2** bay leaves
- **2** garlic cloves, chopped
  salt and pepper to taste

Boil the cleaned ducks in water. Remove from water and cool. Remove all meat from birds and return to a fresh pot of boiling water. Add all other ingredients. Serve when vegetables are cooked. Spices may be added as desired to enhance the flavor.

Ed Anderson
Campbell Ford, Ontario, Canada

Soak Waterfowl Overnight

After cleaning waterfowl, soak the meat in saltwater overnight. You can add a little vinegar to the water to help tenderize the meat.

Brown's Duck Jerky

4-5 mature duck breasts (5 lbs.)
  2 pkgs. meat marinade
  6 T. liquid smoke
  4 T. salt
  2 cups water

Slice the meat into no less than 1/4-inch thick strips. Meat is easier to cut when partially frozen. Combine with remaining ingredients and marinate overnight in a covered container. Dry on racks in oven on very low heat. Put cookie sheet underneath meat to catch drips. Leave oven door slightly open to release moisture.

Troy A. Brown
West Jordan, Utah

When Duck's Done

One of the easiest ways to check a duck for doneness is to stick the breast with a pointed object. If the juice is lightly colored red, the meat is at the medium rare stage. Clear juice means the bird is well done. If no juice comes out, you're in trouble — it's going to be dry!

Duck Jerky

4	duck breasts (mallard size) or 6 smaller
10	oz. teriyaki marinade
5	oz. soy sauce
1	12-oz. can of beer
32	oz. pineapple juice
2	T. garlic powder
2	T. onion powder
2	T. meat tenderizer
2	T. black pepper
1/4	cup sugar
2	T. cracked pepper

Mix all liquid and dry ingredients in large bowl, for marinade. Skin and breast-out ducks, remove meat from breast bone. Cut breast meat into strips 1/4-inch to 3/8-inch thick. Put strips in marinade and refrigerate for 24 to 48 hours.

To cook: Use charcoal smoker with 20 charcoal briquettes, 3-4 wood chunks soaked in water or beer (wood can be apple, hickory or mesquite). You want a very slow fire. Put water pan over coals and fill with marinade. Spray grills with nonstick cooking spray and place first grill over water pan.

Place breast strips in layer on grill and sprinkle with cracked pepper. Place second grill on smoker and fill with meat, sprinkle with cracked pepper. Cover with lid and place wood chunks on coals. Smoke for 2 1/2 hours. Other cooking methods may be used for this recipe – dehydration, gas smoker, oven. Cooking times will vary.

Glen Healey
St. Ann, Missouri

Ken's Wild Goose Breast and Wild Rice Casserole

1	wild goose breast
2	boxes Uncle Ben's original wild rice
1	cup green onions, chopped
1/2	cup green bell pepper, chopped
8-oz.	fresh mushrooms, sliced
2	carrots, shredded
1	T. ADDOBO seasoning
1	T. garlic powder
1	T. Lawry's seasoned salt
1	T. Lawry's seasoned pepper
4	T. butter
1/2	cup dry red wine

Prepare rice according to instructions on box; set aside. Sauté all vegetables in 4 T. butter for 3 minutes. Add vegetables to cooked rice mixture. Add dry seasonings to rice mixture and stir. Fillet goose breast 1/2-inch thick. In a hot skillet, brown fillets in 4 T. butter for 30 seconds on each side. Pour half of the rice mixture in a 9x13x2-inch casserole pan. Arrange goose fillets on rice and cover with remaining mixture. Drizzle wine over all. Bake uncovered in preheated oven at 350 degrees for 20 minutes.

Kenneth W. Fortner
Elizabethton, Tennessee

Plum Sauce Wild Goose

1	5-6-lb. goose
	salt and pepper to taste
2	T. sugar
1 1/4	tsp. salt
1/2	cup plum sauce
3	T. dark soy sauce
4	garlic cloves, crushed
3	green onions, cut in 2-inch pieces
2	large pieces dried orange peel or
1/2	tsp. grated fresh orange peel
1/4	cup sherry
1 1/2	cup cold water

Clean and remove all the fat around the goose cavity. Rub inside with salt and pepper. Mix all remaining ingredients, and pour over goose. Marinate for at least 3 hours. Roast the goose in the sauce at 350 degrees for 20-25 minutes per pound. Turn goose and baste with sauce several times during baking. Add water if the sauce thickens too much, and continue roasting until tender. Lift goose out of the roasting pan and cut in pieces. Keep warm on a hot platter. Skim fat from sauce in roasting pan. Add a little boiling water and sherry, if necessary, to sauce; stir well. Pour over the goose and serve.

Marinated Goose Breast

- **2** 1-lb. goose breasts (or duck)
- **1/3** cup soy sauce
- **1/3** cup olive oil
- **1/4** cup dry red wine
- **1** T. ground green peppercorns

Combine liquids in shallow pan and stir lightly. Place breasts in pan and turn over. Sprinkle green peppercorns over the top. Marinade for 24 hours, turning occasionally.

Sauce:
- **3** T. your favorite jelly or preserve
- **1/3** cup water
- **1/2** tsp. ground caraway seed
- **1** T. Dijon mustard

Combine all ingredients in saucepan and heat slowly until mixed. Continue heating to thicken. Keep warm for serving. Serve rice with meat and sauce. Heat barbecue to high. First sear meat on high, then reduce heat slightly. Meat will puff up. Cook for 5 minutes per side for rare meat, longer for medium or well-done meat. Baste with remaining marinade. Remove from fire and let sit after cooking for a few minutes; then slice meat on an angle. Serve slices over bread or next to rice and pour sauce over meat.

Kevin C. Geenty
Branford, Connecticutt

Roast Goose or Duck

1	4-lb. goose, dressed
4	tsp. salt
2	tsp. ground ginger
2	tsp. dried basil
1	tsp. pepper
2	cups honey + 4 T.
1/2	cup butter
1/4	cup orange juice
3	tsp. lemon juice
2	tsp. grated orange peel
1/4	tsp. dried mustard
2	oranges

Combine salt, ginger, basil, pepper and put half of mixture inside goose; set aside. Heat remaining ingredients except for orange in double boiler. When this mixture is heated and syrupy, rub 3 T. inside goose. Peel oranges and cut into wedges; put inside goose cavity. Add 4 more T. honey to mixture inside goose. Truss legs. Rub remainder of basil mixture on outside of goose and pour honey over goose. Cover with foil. Bake for 2 hours at 375 degrees. Unwrap, baste and cook 30 minutes longer at 325 degrees.

Kevin C. Geenty
Branford, Connecticut

Mud Hen Stew

I   mud hen (coot)
    water
    flour
    vinegar

Clean coot thoroughly and cut in half. Boil in large kettle with enough water to keep meat covered, until tender. Remove coot and save the liquid in kettle.

In large frying pan, brown flour to a medium dark color and slowly add half the liquid, stirring constantly so it doesn't lump. If it lumps, strain as it is boiling before adding to the rest of liquid.

When thoroughly mixed, add vinegar for a slight flavor. Add mud hen and simmer for at least 1/2 hour to give flavor to meat. The stew will be thickened to gravy consistency and should be spooned over potato dumplings.

Cajun Waterfowl with Creole Sauce

I   **goose or duck breast**
    milk and egg for dipping

Coating:
   3/8   **portion flour**
   1/4   **portion bread crumbs**
   1/4   **portion corn meal**
   1/8   **portion "Tony Chachere's Creole Seasonings"**

Soak the waterfowl breast in milk for a few hours.
Pound the breast using a wooden mallet, skin side up.
Cut the breast into bite-sized pieces.

Prepare deep fryer (about 350-degree oil) and coating.
Dip in milk/egg mixture then flour coating, then fry
for about 10 minutes per batch.

Small Game

Porcupine
Rabbit
Squirrel
Woodchuck

Fried Porcupine

1	porcupine
1½	cups flour
¼	lb. butter

Cook the porcupine meat in a pressure cooker for 45 minutes then let cool. Remove meat from the bones, roll meat in flour and fry in butter until brown. Recipe also works for rabbit or woodchuck.

Kevin Avery
Ashland, New Hampshire

Substituting All-Purpose Flour

In any recipe calling for self-rising flour, you can substitute 1 cup all-purpose flour, plus 1 teaspoon baking powder, plus ½ teaspoon salt for every cup of self-rising flour called for in the recipe.

Barbecue Wild Rabbit

1	rabbit, cut up
1	medium onion
2	T. vinegar
4	T. brown sugar
1/4	tsp. pepper
1	cup catsup
1	cup water
3	T. Worcestershire sauce
1/2	tsp. ground mustard
1/2	cup diced celery or 1 T. celery salt

Boil rabbit with onions until tender. Brown meat and onions in shortening. Mix together rest of ingredients and pour over rabbit. Bake at 350 degrees for 3 hours.

Larry Hitchcock
Prairie du Sac, Wisconsin

Using Drawn Butter

Any time you fry or saute in butter, use drawn butter to avoid browning, smoking and splattering. Drawn butter is easily made by melting solid butter over low heat in a sauce pan until it is completely melted, and the solids separate from the liquids. Remove from heat and let stand until it cools slightly, then pour off the top portion—the liquid butter fat—and use it for frying. This is also referred to as clarified butter in some recipes.

Myron's Marinated Rabbit

3-4   lbs. rabbit, fresh or frozen
 1   large onion, cut up
 1/2 large green pepper, cut up
 1-2 celery stalks, sliced
 2   garlic cloves, chopped
     salt and pepper to taste
 1/2 tsp. oregano
 1   T. dry parsley (or several fresh sprigs)
 3   T. catsup/tomato sauce
     cayenne pepper to taste
 1   cup liquid (sauterne, cider, tomato sauce or water)

Soak fresh or frozen rabbit overnight in marinade. Cut up meat and brown with vegetables in hot skillet for 5 to 10 minutes. Place all meat and other ingredients in slow cooker. Cover and cook on low for 8 to 10 hours. (Dry red apples plus 1/4 cup brown sugar may be used in place of the 1 cup liquid.)

Myron F. Green
Mena, Arizona

Peachy Rabbit

2   lbs. rabbit parts
2   T. shortening
1   can cream of chicken soup
1/4   cup water
1/4   tsp. poultry seasoning
6   canned peach halves, drained

In skillet, brown rabbit in shortening. Pour off fat. Add remaining ingredients except peaches. Cover and simmer for 45 minutes or until tender. Add peaches and heat.

Tom Kohler
Payson, Utah

**Nutrition Label
What it means**

Sugar Free: Less than 0.5 grams of sugar per serving.

Country-Style Rabbit

1	2 to 2½ lb. rabbit, cut into 8 pieces
¼	lb. butter
½	cup flour
1	tsp. salt
½	tsp. black pepper
¼	tsp. cayenne pepper
½	cup dry white wine
	creamy gravy (recipe follows)

Melt butter in heavy skillet over medium heat. Mix flour, salt, pepper and cayenne in paper or plastic bag. Shake rabbit pieces in flour mixture to coat, then brown well in hot butter, turning to brown evenly on both sides. Remove rabbit to heavy, casserole dish, add wine, cover and bake at 325 degrees for 45 minutes to one hour. When rabbit is tender, remove to heated platter and pour any liquid remaining in pan into creamy gravy and cook, stirring over medium heat to desired consistency. Serve with mashed potatoes, rice or noodles, and creamy gravy.

Creamy Gravy:

2	T. flour
1	cup milk
	pan drippings

Add flour to pan drippings remaining in pan rabbit was cooked in. Cook, stirring over medium heat until flour is cooked but not browned. Add milk and cook, stirring over medium heat until thickened.

Rabbit Pot Pie

1 wild rabbit, cooked
2 cans cream of potato soup
1 can cream of chicken soup
1 can mixed peas and carrots, drained
2 pie crusts

De-bone and chunk the cooked rabbit. Mix soups together with peas and carrots. Heat thoroughly. Add rabbit chunks. Line 10-inch pie plate with pie crust. Put in rabbit mixture and top with other pie crust. Bake at 350 degrees until mixture is bubbly and pie crust is brown.

Dale Olson
Elroy, Wisconsin

**Nutrition Label
What it means**

High Fiber: Five grams of fiber (or more) per serving.

V-8 Rabbit

2 rabbits
   water
1/4 lb. margarine
2 cups flour
1-2 qts. V-8 juice (regular or spicy)

Cut rabbit into pieces and place in large pot or Dutch oven. Cover with water and bring to boil for 20 minutes. Drain water and remove rabbit from pot. Replace pot on stove and add margarine.

Roll pieces of rabbit in flour and brown in margarine. When all pieces have been browned, replace them all in pot and cover with V-8 juice. Heat to boiling, then reduce heat to simmer.

Cover and simmer 1 to 1½ hours. Remove rabbit. Add water to leftover flour and use to thicken V-8 juice for gravy. Serve gravy over rice or potatoes.

LaVern Noyce
Vassar, Michigan

Beer Rabbit

    4   rabbits, cleaned and cut up
    2   cans beer
    4   potatoes, chopped
    2   carrots, sliced
    2   celery stalks, sliced
    I   onion, chopped
    I   tsp. salt
        pepper to taste

Place all ingredients, except beer, in roasting pan. Put
pepper on top to taste. Pour beer over ingredients.
Cover and bake for 3 hours at 300 degrees.

**Nutrition Label
What it means**

Good Source of Fiber: There are 2.5 to 4.9
grams of fiber per serving.

Smothered Rabbit

3-4 lbs. rabbit
cooking oil or shortening
flour to coat meat
salt and pepper to taste
1 large onion, sliced
2 10½-oz. cans cream
of mushroom soup
1 soup can of milk
3-4 oz. wine

Heat oil in deep skillet. Dredge meat with seasoned flour and brown in skillet. Add sliced onion.

Pour soup, milk and wine over meat and simmer for 1½ hours or until tender.

H.G. "Doug" Douglas
Huntsville, Arkansas

Squirrel Bake

 2 squirrels, cleaned and cut up
 I onion, chopped
 1/2 green pepper, seeded and chopped
 I tsp. dry mustard
 1/4 tsp. thyme
 1/4 tsp. basil
 1/4 cup brown sugar
 1/2 cup red wine (or substitute fruit juice)
 1/4 cup red wine vinegar
   flour
   butter

Coat squirrel pieces with flour, then brown in butter and remove to plate. Sauté onion and green pepper in butter. In bowl, mix onions, green pepper and remaining ingredients thoroughly. Place browned squirrel pieces in casserole dish and cover with sauce.

Bake at 325 degrees for approximately 1 hour.

Barbecued Squirrel

2-4   squirrels, cleaned and quartered
1/4   cup wine vinegar
6   T. ketchup
2   T. celery, finely chopped
3   T. steak sauce
1   cup vegetable oil
1/3   cup red wine (or substitute fruit juice)
1   small onion, chopped
1   garlic clove, finely chopped
1   T. lemon juice
    cayenne pepper to taste
    salt to taste

Combine all sauce ingredients in pan and simmer for 15 minutes, stirring frequently. Baste squirrels with sauce and allow to sit for 15 minutes. Grill over charcoal and turn every 5 to 7 minutes, basting with sauce each time. Continue until squirrels are cooked to your liking.

Baked Squirrel

2   squirrels, halved
1/2   tsp. salt
1   tsp. black pepper
1   bottle Italian dressing

Place squirrel halves in a shallow baking pan, add salt, pepper, and Italian dressing. Marinate for 4-5 hours. Place squirrel with marinade uncovered in oven at 350 degrees for 45-50 minutes or until done.

Restoring The Crisp

To restore crispness in salad greens, put them in a bowl, cover with cold water, add a few ice cubes and 1 or 2 teaspoons of vinegar, then stir. Let sit for at least 15 minutes, drain, rinse and serve.

Paprika Squirrel

- 4 squirrels, cleaned and washed
  water
  salt and pepper to taste
- 2 T. oil
- 1 cup onion, chopped
- 1 T. paprika
- 1/4 cup white wine
- 1/4 cup condensed chicken broth
- 1/2 cup sour cream

Quarter the squirrels, then place in pressure cooker with an inch of water. Bring to pressure and cook for about 15 minutes. Cool under running water and remove lid. Remove all meat from bones. Season with salt and pepper. Brown squirrel in 1-2 T. hot oil. Remove squirrel. Add one cup of chopped onion to the pan and sauté until translucent, but not brown. Stir in paprika. Stir the squirrel back in, coating all pieces evenly. Add white wine and chicken broth. Bring to boil, cover and simmer for 30 minutes. Remove squirrel meat with a slotted spoon. Reduce the pan contents to 1/2 cup by boiling, then slowly stir in 1/2 cup sour cream. Return squirrel meat to sauce and reheat (not to boiling). Serve over hot, cooked noodles with homemade biscuits. Sprinkle with extra paprika for color.

Ronald M. Tussel, Jr.
Hawley, Pennsylvania

Squirrels and Dumplings

4-6 squirrels, cleaned and halved
¹/₂ cup carrots, chopped
¹/₂ cup celery, chopped
¹/₂ cup onion, chopped
water
flour
salt and pepper to taste

Put squirrels in Dutch oven, cover with water and bring to a boil. Reduce heat and simmer until squirrels are tender. After squirrels have cooked approximately 15 minutes, add carrots, celery and onion. Remove pot from heat, remove squirrels and take all meat from the bones. Return meat to broth.

To make dumplings, put one cup of flour into a bowl, add a pinch of salt and slowly add water until flour is thick enough to knead. On a floured surface, roll dough until approximately 1/8-inch thick. Slice into strips and cut into approximately 2-inch lengths. Bring the broth to a boil and drop the dough strips into the broth. Add salt and pepper to taste. Continue to boil broth until dough is cooked, approximately 5 to 7 minutes.

Shake & Bake Woodchuck

- I **woodchuck**
  cold water
- ¹/₂ **cup baking soda**
- I **pkg. Shake & Bake (your favorite flavor)**
  garlic powder to taste
- I **egg**
  sage (optional)
  apple slices (optional)

Remove the glands under the legs that look like kidneys. Cut woodchuck into quarters and soak in cold
water with ¹/₂ cup baking soda for 1 hour. Pat dry.
Place Shake & Bake in a brown bag, adding more garlic
to taste. Beat one egg in a bowl, then roll the woodchuck pieces in the beaten egg. Drop into bag; shake
until thoroughly covered. Place pieces on a rack in a
300-degree oven until meat is tender, and coating has
turned brown. Approximate cooking time is 1¹/₂ hours
depending on the age of the woodchuck. Younger
chucks are more tender. For older chucks, coat the
meat with salt, pepper, garlic powder and a little sage.
Roll the pieces in flour and place in a roasting bag. A
few apple slices will add moisture. Add your favorite
gravy for serving.

Ronald M. Tussel, Jr.
Hawley, Pennsylvania

Michael's Woodchuck Chunks

2-3　woodchucks or groundhogs
　　　meat tenderizer
　　　cooking oil
　　　salt and pepper to taste
　　　spices to taste
　　　garlic powder to taste, or blackened seasoning
　　　Italian flavored bread crumbs
　2　eggs

Clean and skin woodchucks, removing the meat from the bones. Remove all fat and glands. Cut meat into bite-sized chunks. Sprinkle meat tenderizer onto chunks. Mix oil and spices into bowl, stir well. Add meat. Place lid on bowl and shake well to mix ingredients. Place bowl in refrigerator for 1-3 hours or until chilled. Pour bread crumbs onto plate, stir eggs in a bowl and place next to bread crumbs . Remove chunks from bowl, dip into eggs, and roll in bread crumbs. Pour oil into frying pan or deep fryer. Over medium heat, place chunks in oil, cook until light brown (5-10 minutes) turning often. Remove chunks from oil and place on paper towels to drain off excess oil.

Michael F. Sestak
Erie, Pennsylvania

Hunter's Stew

2 lbs. small game meat, cut into small pieces
3 medium potatoes, cut into 1-inch cubes
1 large onion, diced to small pieces
4 large carrots, cut into small pieces
1/2 medium-sized turnip, cut into 1-inch cubes
1 heaping T. flour
1 level tsp. salt
1/4 tsp. black pepper
1 qt. cold water

Place meat in an 8- or 9-inch pot. Add remaining ingredients, stir and simmer for 1 hour over low heat.

Welton Ernst
Lan Co. Nova Scotia, Canada

Salads, etc.

Salads
Soups
Appetizers
Side Dishes

King's Sauce

2	gal. ripe or canned whole tomatoes, peeled and chopped
1	pt. vinegar
1½	cup sugar
30-40	jalapeno peppers, seeded and chopped
4-6	bell peppers, seeded and chopped
1	qt. onion (yellow or white), chopped
1½	tsp. pickling spice (put in bag and boil separately, then pour over sauce)
1	cup celery, chopped
2	T. sweet basil
2	tsp. cloves (optional)
	salt to taste

Cook all ingredients in large pot over low heat until desired thickness is reached. Keep refrigerated. Seal in jars for future use.

Lloyd King
Liberty, Mississippi

King's Biscuits

4	cups Bisquick
8	oz. sour cream
1	can 7-up
1	stick butter or margarine

Mix Bisquick and sour cream. Add enough 7-up to mix and roll or cut Bisquick. Melt butter or margarine in pan and pour over Bisquick after rolled. Heat oven to 400 degrees and bake for 20-25 minutes.

Lloyd King
Liberty, Mississippi

Velvety Walnut Soup

2	T. butter or margarine
I	onion, diced
3	medium-sized potatoes, diced
I ½	T. flour
I ½	pints water
½	pint whipped cream
3 ½	oz. walnut halves, diced (keep four halves for decoration)
I ½	tsp. salt
3-4	oz. whipped cream
	pepper to taste
	nutmeg to taste
	chervil leaves

Heat butter or margarine in a pan. Add onion and heat. Add potatoes, cook for 1 minute and add flour. Add water and cream, cook on low heat for 30 minutes. Blend with mixer and return to pan. Stir in walnuts and serve in soup bowls, adding whipped cream on top. Add pepper and nutmeg to taste. Place chervil leaves and a walnut half on top of the whipped cream.

Cumberland Sauce

¹/₂	medium orange
¹/₂	medium lemon
¹/₂	pint water
3	soupspoons of red currant jelly
¹/₄	pint of port (or sherry or red wine)
¹/₂	juice of I orange
¹/₂	juice of I lemon
I	small pinch of cayenne pepper
I	pinch of salt

Peel fruit and cut into very thin strips. Bring water to a boil, put in lemon and orange strips for 5 minutes, rinse quickly under cold water, then set aside. Heat jelly in a small pan until liquified, remove from heat. Add wine, mix and pour into a tureen. Add juice of ¹/₂ orange and ¹/₂ lemon, pinch of cayenne pepper and salt. Verify taste, add the orange and lemon strips, refrigerate for 30 minutes before serving.

Frank N. Vallotton
Morgas, Switzerland

Fiddlehead Ferns

I	lb. fiddleheads
2	beef bouillon cubes
I	pinch garlic
I	tsp. seasoned salt

Combine ingredients and cook until tender, for about 30 minutes.

Ken Robinson
Springfield, Maine

Pumpkin Soup

1	T. of butter or margarine
1	T. of curry
1 ½	lb. pumpkin, diced (without the skin)
7	oz. of vegetable stock
2	T. fresh pumpkin seeds (without the shells, or purchased unsalted)
	chervil leaves

Heat butter or margarine in a pan, add curry. Add pumpkin, cook for 1 minute. Add vegetable stock, cover and cook. When cooked, beat with mixer. Put back in pan and add salt and pepper to taste. Add vegetable stock if needed to "lighten" the soup. Serve and sprinkle with fresh broken pumpkin seed and decorate with some chervil leaves.

Frank N. Vallotton
Morgas, Switzerland

Noodles and Cabbage

6	slices of bacon, cut into thirds
1	head of cabbage, cored and chopped
1	package frozen egg noodles
	salt and pepper to taste

In a Dutch oven, fry the bacon until almost crisp. Add the cabbage to the pot, stir well and cover. Cook until cabbage is soft. In a separate pan, cook egg noodles according to directions and drain. When cabbage is done to your liking, add noodles and stir completely. Add salt and pepper to taste and serve as a side dish with any wild game.

Brussels Sprouts and Apples

1   T. butter or margarine
    Brussels sprouts
1   tsp. fennel seeds
2½ oz. vegetable stock
2   unpeeled firm red apples, cut into thin strips
    salt and pepper to taste

Heat butter or margarine in a large saucepan. Add the brussels sprouts and the fennel seeds, cook for 1 minute. Wet with vegetable stock and cook at low heat for 15 minutes. Add apple strips, heat 2 minutes, add salt and pepper and serve.

Frank N. Valotton
Morgas, Switzerland

Braised Endives

2   endives
1   T. olive oil
1   tsp. curry
1   tsp. lemon juice
½   tsp. salt
1   small tomato, diced
    minced parsley
    fresh ground pepper

Cut a cone out of the base of the endive, cut in half the long way, making sure to keep enough endive around the cone so as not to lose the leaves. Put each half, cut side up, in a greased baking dish. Mix the oil, curry, lemon juice and salt; brush onto the endives. Cook for 15 to 30 minutes in the center of a hot oven at 425 degrees. Take out of the oven, cover with the diced tomato, parsley and pepper.

Frank N. Vallotton
Morgas, Switzerland

Low-Sugar Applesauce Cake

2	cups raisins	I	tsp. baking soda
2	cups water	2	cups flour
I	cup unsweetened applesauce	1 1/2	tsp. cinnamon
		1/2	tsp. nutmeg
4	egg whites	I	tsp. vanilla
2	T. Equal or Sweet 'n Low	I	cup nuts
3/4	cup oil		

Preheat oven to 350 degrees. Cook raisins in water until the water evaporates. Add applesauce, eggs, sweetener and oil mix. Blend in baking soda, flour, cinnamon, nutmeg and vanilla. Pour in an 8-inch cake pan and bake for 30 minutes. Garnish with nuts.

Kenneth W. Crummett
Sugar Grove, West Virginia

Potato Dumplings

3 cups mashed potatoes
2 eggs
 flour

Mash 3 cups potatoes and cool (instant mashed potatoes will work). Add 2 eggs and mix thoroughly. Add enough flour to shape into firm balls sized between golf and tennis balls. Drop balls into large kettle boiling water (stir occasionally so they don't stick to bottom) and cook for at least 1/2 hour (longer doesn't hurt them). Serve hot. Cut dumplings on plate and cover with mud hen stew, thick stew juice and mud hen halves.

Polenta Parmesan

     2   cups yellow cornmeal
  4¹/₄ cups water
     I   tsp. salt
     4   T. butter
   ¹/₂ cup Parmesan cheese, grated

In Dutch oven, add salt to the water and bring to a boil. Slowly add cornmeal to water while stirring. After all cornmeal is stirred into water, whisk briskly for 30 seconds to break up all lumps.

Cornmeal mixture must be stirred almost continuously to avoid scorching. Cook for approximately 30 minutes, add butter and Parmesan cheese. Pour cornmeal onto a large surface, such as a cookie sheet and spread evenly. Allow to cool. Cut the polenta into squares or other shapes as desired.

In saucepan, melt 2 T. butter. Fry polenta shapes in butter until golden brown on both sides. Sprinkle lightly with Parmesan cheese and serve.

Mike Vail
Plymouth, Minnesota

Norfolk Oyster Stew

    1   quart oysters, unwashed after shucking
    1/2 cup water
    1/2 cup half-and-half or light cream
    1/4 cup butter
        salt and pepper to taste

The fresher the oysters, the better this will taste. Shucking your own oysters is best and after shucking, do not wash them, as you will remove a lot of the salty taste.

Put the oysters, water and butter in a pan and bring to a boil. Cook until the oysters begin to curl on the edges; they'll almost look like little raviolis. Reduce heat, add the cream and stir. Add salt and pepper to taste. Simmer for a few minutes (do not bring to a boil) and serve.

Mike Vail
Plymouth, Minnesota

Noodles Au Gratin

    2   cups egg noodles   1/2 cup grated
        water   Parmesan cheese
        salt   1/4 tsp. ground nutmeg
    4   T. butter

Bring a pot of water to boil. Add some salt and the raw noodles. Cook noodles until tender. Drain noodles and toss with the Parmesan cheese and nutmeg. Place noodles in a buttered baking dish, cover with more grated cheese and sprinkle with melted butter. Bake at 400 degrees in oven until brown, then serve.

Liberty Loaf

2   cups self-rising cornmeal
2   T. baking powder
2   eggs, beaten
1/2   cup oil
1/2   bell pepper, chopped
2   hot peppers, chopped
1   6-oz. can creamed corn
1   bunch green onions, chopped
1   cup sour cream (8 oz.)
3   oz. cheddar cheese

Mix dry ingredients together and add eggs. Sauté vegetables in oil. Add sour cream. Combine all ingredients. Turn onto a bread board and form into a loaf. Place loaf in a bread pan or on a baking sheet. Sprinkle cheddar cheese over loaf and bake for 25-30 minutes at 375 degrees or until brown.

Lloyd H. King
Liberty, Mississippi

German Beans

4   strips bacon, chopped
1   large onion, chopped
2   cups fresh green beans, cut into pieces
2   large tomatoes, seeded and chopped
1   tsp. white vinegar
    salt and pepper to taste
1/2   cup water

Fry bacon in saucepan until crisp. Remove bacon pieces and drain on a paper towel. Add onions to bacon grease left in skillet and sauté gently until clear. To skillet add beans, tomatoes, vinegar, salt, pepper and water.

Stir everything together and cover pan. Bring to a boil, then lower heat and simmer for 15 minutes. Remove cover and add bacon. Stir and serve.

Mike Vail
Plymouth, Minnesota

French Potatoes

> white potatoes
> butter
> salt and pepper to taste

Using a melon baller, cut small ball shapes from potatoes. Fry over medium heat in butter until browned on all sides. Place in a warm serving bowl. Season to taste.

Morel Sauce

I   package 1/2 oz. dried morels or 5 1/2 oz. fresh
     morels
     Water
     Milk
I   onion, minced
I   T. butter or margarine
I   tsp. Herbs of Provence (mixed)
2   oz. port or sherry wine
6 1/2   oz. cream for sauce
     salt and fresh ground pepper

Immerse the dried morels for 2 hours in cold water and milk. Dry the morels, cut in half and rinse. If fresh, wash, cut in half and wash again. Sprinkle onion into hot butter or margarine, add Herbs of Provence and morels. Cover and heat (to braise); and wet with wine, add cream and bring to a boil. Let simmer to thicken sauce. Salt and pepper to taste.

Frank N. Vallotton
Morgas, Switzerland

Sour Cream Mushrooms

1	lb. fresh mushrooms, sliced
1	onion, chopped
3	T. butter
3	T. flour
1/2	tsp. Worcestershire sauce
1/2	tsp. garlic, minced
1	cup sour cream
	toast

In skillet, melt butter and cook onion until lightly browned. Reduce heat, add mushrooms to skillet and cook for 8 to 10 minutes until mushrooms are soft. Sift flour completely over mushrooms and stir well, coating the mushrooms. Add Worcestershire sauce and sour cream, stirring well. Cook for 5 minutes and serve poured over toast.

Mushroom Duxelles

Per serving:

2	cups mushrooms, finely chopped
1	medium onion, chopped
1	large shallot, chopped
	salt and pepper to taste
1/4	tsp. ground nutmeg
1/4	cup butter

Melt butter in saucepan over medium heat. Add all other ingredients and cook down until ingredients have browned and all liquids have evaporated. Serve as side dish to any wild game meat.

Refreshing Anchovy Vinaigrette

Vinaigrette, for each serving of salad:

3   T. olive oil
1   T. wine vinegar
1   tsp. dijon mustard
1/2 tsp. minced garlic
    salt and pepper to taste

    anchovy fillets
    capers
    milk
    croutons

For each serving: cover four anchovy fillets with milk and soak for about an hour to desalt, stirring occasionally. Drain the anchovies, pat dry. Combine a teaspoon of capers with the anchovies and crush to a smooth paste. Whisk this mixture into the vinaigrette, blending thoroughly.

Pour over mixed greens, preferably romaine. Add croutons as desired.

Venison Salad

Per serving:

3-4	thin slices cooked venison
1/2	cup white wine
1	T. olive oil
1	T. fresh basil, chopped
2-3	boiled new potatoes, thinly sliced
1	tomato, thinly sliced
3-4	thin slices white onion

Vinaigrette per serving:

3	T. olive oil
1	T. wine vinegar
1	tsp. dijon mustard
	salt and pepper to taste

While potatoes are still warm, arrange slices on plate and cover with wine and olive oil. Sprinkle with basil. Gently turn slices to coat with liquid. Allow potatoes to sit for about 10 minutes.

Build potatoe slices into a mound and surround with strips of venison, followed by tomatoes, then onions. Pour vinaigrette over entire dish and serve.

Tomatoes Mozzarella

Per serving:

- 1   medium ripe tomato, thinly sliced
- 2   oz. mozzarella cheese, thinly sliced
- 1   tsp. fresh basil, chopped
- 1/2 tsp. wine vinegar
- 1   T. olive oil
      salt and pepper to taste

Arrange tomato slices on salad plate and cover with mozzarella. Sprinkle with remaining ingredients and serve at room temperature.

Avocado and Cucumber Salad

Per serving:

- 1/2 ripe avocado, seeded and diced
- 1/2 cucumber, sliced lengthwise
- 1   tsp. basil, chopped
- 1/2 tsp. garlic, minced

Vinaigrette:

- 3   T. olive oil
- 1   T. wine vinegar
- 2   tsp. dijon mustard
      salt and pepper to taste

Slice cucumber and toss together with avocado. Sprinkle with basil and garlic, salt and pepper. Pour vinaigrette over and mix well.

Indexes

Recipes
Contributing Members

© ANDERSON...

Contributing Members

Reaver, Mark
  London, OH, 93
Reeges, Howard W., Jr.
  Butler, PA, 73
Robinson, Ken
  Springfield, ME, 208
Roman, David B.
  Chicago, IL, 53
Runde, David
  Teutopolis, IL, 146
Salisbury, John H.
  Green River, WY, 101, 140
Sestak, Michael F.
  Erie, PA, 165, 203
Sethna, K.K.
  Ashville, OH, 43
Shipton, Bill
  Las Cruces, MN
Small, Melissa
  Reno, NV, 147
Stammen, Juleen
  Palermo, ND, 46
Stevenson, Terry
  Leadville, OH, 54, 55,
  72, 118
Strickbine, Steve
  Bartlesville, OK, 64
Swihart, Dick
  San Mateo, CA, 89, 163
Tantlinger, Terry
  New Kensington, PA, 44
Taylor, Steve
  Edwardsville, KS, 162, 166
Thompson, Christine
  Odin, IL, 167
Trost, Richard
  Vernon, NY, 61
Tussel, Ronald M., Jr.
  Hawley, PA, 35, 36, 141,
  200, 202

Tyson, William E., Jr.
  Toxey, AL, 86
Vail, Mike
  Plymouth, MN, 212,
  213, 215
Vaira, Barbara A.
  Wilmington, IL, 103
Vallotton, Frank N.
  Morgas, Switzerland, 102,
  208, 209, 210
Vath, Tom
  Johnson, IA, 59
VonFeldt, Richard A.
  Larned, KS, 156
Warner, Wayne
  South Zanesville, OH, 51
Weber, Oscar and Joan
  Peoria, IL, 145
Weihert, S.C.
  Wausau, WI, 69, 70
Wells, Louis E.
  Dripping Springs, TX, 120
Wetzel, Andrew J.
  Titusville, FL, 132
Winter, Ronald
  Woodhaven, MI, 110,
  111, 112